AWAKEN

Your Inner

Hero

Volume One

The Hero Intelligence Agency - P.O. Box 14, Camden East, ON Canada K0K 1J0

info@hero-intelligence.com

Ordering Information: Quantity sales. Special discounts are available on quantity purchases by corporations, associations, and others. For details, contact the publisher at the address above. Orders for international trade, bookstores, and wholesalers.

Please contact The Hero Intelligence Agency: Email: info@hero-intelligence.com or visit: www.hero-intelligence.com

Written in Canada

Designed in Canada

Printed in China

Publisher's Cataloging-in-Publication data

A title of a book: Awaken Your Inner Hero ISBN 978-5323-9605-2

1. The main category of the book —Youth Non-Fiction - Children's Book

2. Non-Fiction

First Edition 2018

Designed and Printed by:

JBO Global 5569-47th Street Red Deer, Alberta Canada T4N1S1

jboglobal10x@gmail.com

This book is dedicated **to** HEROES everywhere who **dedicate** their **lives** to creating a safe, *accepting* and compassionate **world.** The HERO in us sees the Hero in YOU!

"A real **Hero** *sees the hero in everyone."*
– JB Owen

"Awaken Your Inner Hero is a rich tapestry of stories that prove our future is bright with young difference makers. As a father, and now grandfather, I look forward to sharing these stories of infinite possibilities and positivity with my family!"
- Rick Hansen, Founder and CEO, Rick Hansen Foundation

"Awaken Your Inner Hero is a beautiful, compassionate book with extraordinary stories of what heroes really are! What's unique and special in all of us makes us all heroes and I'm blessed to know many!!"
- Marnie Schneider, Founder, Keep on Playing Foundation, Author of Football Freddie & Fumble the Dog Series

"A collection of inspiring stories of the uninhibited spirit of youth - their values, kindness, resilience and hope that enable them to unleash their inner heroes."
- Ron Duke, semi-retired C-Suite executive, Director, Mentor, Advisor and Coach

"Outward capabilities differ but inwardly we are all the same. To teach young children to understand this is so powerful. Thank you for this heroic enterprise."
- Wolfgang Sonnenburg, President, Winspiration® Day Association

"The stories of young people, what they are doing and what motivates them to make a difference are a reminder of the power of unbridled passion and creativity and that one person can make a difference – no matter what age."

- Tammy Moore, CEO, ALS Canada

Awaken

"I found the "*Awaken Your Inner Hero* Book" a fantastic read and absolutely amazing to see the future is in good hands with our youth of today! The stories captured my attention throughout each of their journeys. These young individuals show passion, compassion, inner strength and determination, all important attributes for leadership."
- Kerry Goulet, Global Director of Stop Concussions Foundation

"*Awaken Your Inner Hero* is an invaluable and inspiring collection of the stories of real people who are the role models needed to be most visible in the world in any Era. When I was growing up my father used to tell me stories about inspiring heroes just before I fell asleep at night. With this book, the immense positive effect my father had on me that way can be shared by everyone on Earth using this book. In retrospect how did we as a civilization never produce this book before?"
- Bill Harvey, Executive Director, The Human Effectiveness Institute

"Hearing the young passionate voices behind these stories is truly awe inspiring. I see everyday that our children care passionately about making a difference in this world, wanting to both become children of the world and are willing to work hard to reach their goals. It is our job to both open the world to them and be "guides on the side" giving them the knowledge, tools, opportunities and empowerment to "fly."
- Renalee Gore, Principal at Knowlton Academy,
Eastern Townships School Board

"Everybody has a hero inside, everyone has the capacity when they face their "personal plane crash" in their life to summon their inner most resources to not only survive but grow and thrive! *Awaken your inner Hero* will open your eyes to those resources so your inner hero will be revealed and you will have clarity of your mission on earth.'

- Dave Sanderson, President, Dave Sanderson Speaks International

"I absolutely love "Awaken Your Inner Hero". It's an amazing collection of stories that I cannot wait to share! With our crazy busy lives, I really appreciate the format which allows you to dip in and get some daily inspiration in small digestible pieces. These kids are incredible, and they prove that the future is very bright."

Scott MacGregor, Founder & CEO of SomethingNew LLC and Author of "Standing O!"

"There are books that you read and there are books that inspire action. *Awaken Your Inner Hero* inspires action no matter what you are going through, to be the S/hero of your story. Incredible stories of transformation and how they turned adversity into success."

- Tahani Aburaneh, Founder of Tahani International Inc.

"I have dedicated the past 30 years to mentoring and creating a positive impact on the lives of youth. To read stories of youth who are going out into the world and taking action elevates my belief that mentoring works and is needed around the world."

- Kevin Singleton, Founder & Chief Mentor of Elevate New York

Awaken Your Inner Hero

With foreword by Severn Cullis-Suzuki

Inspiring Stories of Youth Heroes Across Canada
Their Mentors, Teachers, Coaches & Influencers

Tammy Vallieres | Jen Fitzpatrick | Susan Howson
Edited by Anastasia Saluk

CONTENTS

Intelligence

I have worked my whole life to shift people's perspectives from a globalized unsustainable way of living.

I'm a mother, with two little boys who I am teaching to love the Earth too. I've done many things in my life toward my cause, but what people are most inspired by is a speech I gave as a 12-year-old to the UN, asking adults to change their ways. The video of this speech is on YouTube, and continues to surface today. Why is it still powerful? I believe it speaks to the power of and the need for the voice of youth. Youth have everything at stake, with no political agenda or ulterior motives. Youth can speak with a moral authority that no generation has – they truly are the future, and what adults do today ultimately will affect their world.

Youth can call on us, the older generations, to truly live up to our sacred task: to ensure that the world is healthy for our children to inherit. Today, more than ever, adults need to be reminded of this because our current economic era promotes the opposite: to ignore our values, thus ignoring the future. We operate on quarterly reports, fashion seasons, and three-to-five-year government terms. Who is looking out for future generations? We need the clear, honest voice of youth to remind us of what is truly at stake, and of our true responsibility to the future. This is why the voices of the youth in this book matter. They are using their voices to call for change, and are showing the way with their actions.

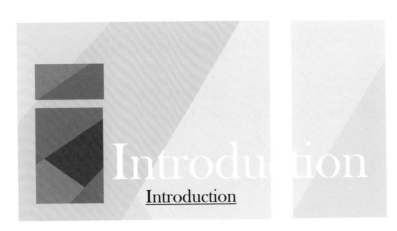

Introduction

Life is like a treasure map, a journey to discover the gems, jewels and treasures that are within every one of us. Each child has a unique contribution to make, and adults should support children in recognizing their own extraordinary potential and actualizing it in the world.

We have been gifted the opportunity to come together and share inspirational stories from youth heroes across Canada. Youth have an innate ability to be authentic and honest, and this book is the vehicle to show us the path to a better world.

We all have a story, and we encourage you to discover yours and awaken your own inner hero!

Tammy Vallieres, Jenny Fitz, and Susan Howson
Co-Founders of the Hero Intelligence Agency

The Hero Intelligence Agency was created to provide a safe space for youth to share their stories, ideas, and superpowers in order to create positive change. Our vision is to call upon YOUth from around the world to awaken their inner heroes and discover their magnificence.

How to Deal with Bad Thoughts

A Story to Help Children by James John

You know how we have so many thoughts during the day? Well, some are good thoughts, and some are bad thoughts, and they come to visit us.

The good ones make us think thoughts of kindness and love towards our family, friends and pets, and that makes us feel good.

But, some days, we think bad thoughts of hating or making fun of someone, or even bullying them, and that makes us feel sad.

Well, there's a special secret that you should know – that the voice in your head that says the bad things is not really you. Grown-ups call it the "ego", and it makes us say and do bad things. This works the same for grown-ups too.

You may even have a name for it or even see it sometimes. It may be dark with a slimy shape. It may trick you and even tell you, "It's really you", when it's really not you.

You came from love, and love would never, ever want to hurt anyone. So, if you are thinking good and loving thoughts, well, that is you.

If you are thinking bad and mean thoughts, well, that is the ego.

So, how do we get these bad thoughts out of our head? We send the ego love. If we come from love, then we should love all creations, good and bad.

Imagine that you are in a dark room and you light a candle. What would happen? It would become bright and there would be no more darkness. That's what you can do when you have the dark thoughts in your head: send it your love. Your love is the light, so the

darkness cannot remain dark anymore. This lets your happy thoughts continue to shine through.

If you have a name for your ego, send it love. If you see the ego, send it love.

So, the next time the ego is giving you bad thoughts, you will know what to do. Send it love. When you send love to the ego, it will start to disappear like magic and then you will think good thoughts again.

Remember, you are a good person who is still learning and may think bad thoughts sometimes. Just send the ego love when it visits. And most importantly, never forget that you were made from love. You are love, and you are loved.

James John
Founder of Love, Appreciate, Forgive
(LAF)

Chapter 1:

I AM AN UPSTANDER

Name: Teagan Adams - **Age:** 16
Hometown: Kelowna, British Columbia

"Remember there's no such thing as a small act of kindness. Every act
creates a ripple with no logical end."

Scott Adams

MY DREAM

When I was 9-years-old, my mom gave my two brothers and I each a toonie and a challenge: to use that money to make more money, and then give that money to charity. At
first I was confused – how could I magically make more money appear from two dollars?
But I learned that, with a bit of money and your own creativity, you really *can* turn a little
money into a lot. I used that toonie to buy supplies to start a lemonade stand, while my
one brother did a magic show and the other did a bake sale. Together, as well as through
several bottle drives as a family, we raised $11,000 in under a year, and that money was
used to build a school in Kenya, Africa. That simple toonie challenge in the summer of
2011 sparked a chain reaction that led me to where I am today.

MY SUPERPOWER IS PLAYING CARDS

A year after the toonie challenge, I was playing with my Pokémon cards when I got an idea for a card game that I called Doogoods. The cards look like Pokémon cards in that each card has a character on it that I came up with, but instead of attacks there are challenges relating to simple acts of kindness, and instead of Hit Points, or HP, there are points to be earned upon the completion of the challenge. It's not a sit-down card game, but rather an active game that is played over time and can be played in a lot of different ways, both in the home and in the classroom. One way that people can use the cards is to simply pick one card each in their family and focus on that card for the week. If you are looking for a little friendly competition, you could independently complete as many of the cards as you can in a certain amount of time while keeping track of your points, and then compare with your friends and family. Basically the whole idea is to get kids having fun while completing simple acts of kindness.

A little while after I came up with Doogoods I heard that *Dragons' Den* auditions were coming to Kelowna. I decided to audition, partly because I was confident in my idea, but also because, as a 10-year-old kid, I thought it would be cool to say that I was on a national television show! My audition was a success, so I was flown to Toronto where I pitched to the Den, and I walked out with a deal with four of the five Dragons: Arlene Dickinson, Bruce Croxon, David Chilton, and Jim Treliving!

Since then I have given a TEDx Talk on my story, and I offer the Doogoods Assembly Program to elementary schools. It is a full program that includes a pack of Doogoods cards for each class, a teaching manual, and five assemblies that I present throughout the academic year about kindness, courage, respect, responsibility, and positive thinking.

I am really proud of the things that I have been able to accomplish so far in my life, as well as the impact that I have been able to make, from raising enough money to build a school in Kenya, to being on *Dragons' Den*, to giving a TEDx Talk, to travelling to Nicaragua with my family to feed kids affected by natural disasters, to speaking internationally alongside big names such as Marc Kielburger, to launching my Doogoods app and website!

MY VOICE MATTERS

I know that simple acts of kindness have the power to change the world because anyone can complete them on a consistent basis anytime and anyplace. You don't need to go out of your way to give someone a smile or a compliment, or to hold the door open for someone, but that simple act can mean the world to someone, and it can also start a ripple effect. My goal is to spread this movement of kindness and raise the next generation as upstanders instead of bystanders. If I am able to spread my movement and develop positive habits in kids at a young age, then the next generation will be filled with upstanders, change makers, and innovators who will ultimately change the world for the better.

MY HEROES

I have had lots of people help me along the way and provide me with opportunities, but no one stands out more than my mom. She was my initial inspiration and she was the one who sparked my movement. She is always there if I need a little bit of an extra push. For example, when preparing to pitch my idea on *Dragons' Den*, she constantly helped me practice my pitch, and eventually it got to the point that I was saying my pitch in my sleep!

Marc and Craig Kielburger inspire me because of their work through the WE movement. They have provided education, food, water, and so much more to help the less fortunate. I also admire Gary Vaynerchuk, an entrepreneur and personal brand expert, and Tim Ferriss, author of *The 4-Hour Workweek*. Lastly I look up to motivational speaker, Tony Robbins, who always sees the good in people.

MY ADVICE TO YOUTH

Understand that although you are only one person out of seven billion, you truly can make a difference, and even change the world. You never know what people are going through, but you can always be there to make their day just a little bit better, and that can make all the difference. Don't ever doubt your abilities to change the world, because it starts with you!

To Adults

We must raise the next generation as upstanders instead of bystanders. That is how we can change the world. Lead by example, and do little things that can truly make a big difference. Create an atmosphere where doing good is fun and kindness is cool so that the next generation will grow up developing these positive habits.

"Teagan has had a lot of motivation and drive since he was little. When he was 7-years-old he participated in a colouring contest so that he could win a part in a play. I remember he said, 'When I win this contest, I want to play the part of the wolf.' Part of me thought to tell him that he may not win because he was one of hundreds who had entered the contest, but I held that thought in and kept encouraging him, and he won the contest and played the part of the wolf! Two years later, the same thing happened when he auditioned for *Dragons' Den*: he talked as if his victory was a sure thing, and I never once tried to prepare him for a negative outcome.

"I strongly believe that a lot of Teagan's success has come from the power of his thoughts and his belief in things happening for him. He shows that age has no limits, and he is part of a powerful generation that I believe will make massive positive changes in our world if we support them. People are listening to children and youth across the world, from teenagers speaking out against gun violence in the U.S., to Malala Yousafzai in Pakistan speaking about equal rights to education. We need to encourage children to speak up and say what they feel needs to be said rather than silencing them.

"You can never be too young – or too old – to do anything momentous. The time is *now* to change the world!"

Chantelle Adams
Teagan's mother

"Some of the biggest barriers we face are in our mind. My world changed when my high school coach Bob Redford told me that "nowhere in the definition of an athlete do you need your legs to be one". As a young boy struggling to come to terms with my shattered hopes and dreams after my spinal cord injury these words shifted everything in my attitude. Regardless of our abilities, visible or invisible – we all have the potential to achieve our dreams. Never give up on your dreams. Together anything is possible!"

– Rick Hansen, Founder and CEO, Rick Hansen Foundation

Chapter 2:
I AM GRATEFUL

Name: Sanjana Ambegaonkar - **Age:** 14
Hometown: Mississauga, Ontario

"In a world filled with hate, we must still dare to hope. In a world filled with anger, we must still dare to comfort. In a world filled with despair, we must still dare to dream. And in a world filled with distrust, we must still dare to believe."

Michael Jackson

MY DREAM

In May 2016 I realized that I was not an ordinary child. I was on the Raymond Aaron Transformation Retreat and Cruise to the Bahamas, and I was left in awe after just finishing a session on the concept of appreciation. At that exact moment, I opened My Notes on my iPhone, and simply jotted down things and people I was grateful for at that second. I then realized that I had to do more with that list. I was put on this earth to do something different and make my life worth living for myself and others. Thus began my journey of becoming an author and motivational speaker.

Since then I have written *The Art of Appreciation: How to Appreciate Everything You Have and Take Nothing for Granted*. The valuable concept of appreciation is one of the most important facets in our lives, and I believe that we should live by this concept and use it to make an impact on the world.

My personal vision is to have a life of meaning for myself and others. It is important to me to live my life in a way that shows love for family and friends and even strangers. I postulate to earn respect for myself based on recognition of my accomplishments and abilities, maintaining a sense of appreciation of the beauty of nature, and a sense of humour.

I intend to have a life that includes constant learning and improvement for myself, but that also creates an atmosphere of pleasurable learning and improvement for others. I work with and around people, and it is important to me that they feel that I have helped them in some way – not necessarily that I do a specific good deed, but more that some kindness or wisdom of mine has touched them.

MY SUPERPOWER IS WRITING

I was not very social, and I had to learn to get out of my comfort zone and be more willing to communicate with others. The best way for me to do this was by writing. I can bring the good to the surface in so many people, thus impacting them positively, through my words.

Sometimes I ran into the challenge of "writer's block" when I simply could not put my thoughts into words, and sometimes I could not find motivation to write, instead spending time on leisurely activities. But when I overcame those challenges, I became so grateful for the change I was able to create. Interestingly enough, these challenges weren't overly difficult to overcome. All I had to do was visualize myself as if I had already achieved my goals and was benefitting from all the hard work I put in. Doing this also made me appreciate the journey to achieving my dreams.

Helping people has opened my horizons to connect with people that I never even dreamed of connecting with. My vision has already impacted the world as attendees of my workshops have thanked me for helping them achieve their dreams that they once thought were impossible.

I feel so proud when I meet new people and tell them who I am. Their expressions and body language when I tell them that I am an award-winning author and speaker make me proud to say that I am not an ordinary teen, and I feel that my hard work has paid off and my vision is being achieved. I am also proud of the fact that I hold my own sold-out events, and people actually enjoy learning and being in a like-minded positive community.

MY VOICE MATTERS

I used to despise change, but now I love it, and I wouldn't trade my life for anyone else's. My life is by no means perfect, but I have no right to complain about it. Even with all the strengths and weaknesses I have discovered about myself, I have a hard time wanting to be somebody else. I love where I am in my life, and I cannot wait to see what the next years have waiting for me.

I value making a difference in life and living with integrity. I always encourage people to try and make a difference in this world. If you give even just a little of yourself, you receive a lot in return. Giving is good for the soul, and it makes you better in everything you do.

MY HEROES

I have a lot of heroes, but my most important heroes are my mom and dad. They gave me my life, my name, and my values, and they helped me become who I am today. They are the ones who took care of me when I was sick, sad, or frightened at night when I was young. Above all, my parents are the ones who will always love me and who will always be there for me when I need them.

MY ADVICE TO YOUTH

Make use of the time you have on this earth. Live your own life instead of someone else's. And most importantly: be brave enough to follow your heart. Let us create a dent in the universe through a movement to help more individuals discover themselves and enrich their universe.

To Adults

Listen to kids – actually listen. Yes, they might be saying stuff that you already know, but if you actually get into the habit of being a good listener, you are going to improve your relationship with them.

"My wife, Swapna, and I have been involved in the personal development industry for the last 20 years. As a coach, I have always emphasized the importance of knowing who you are and what you are put on this earth to do. Once you discover your passion, set focused goals, and take massive action, you really are unstoppable. We value core principles of honesty, integrity, trustworthiness, consistency, creativity and impact, and we imparted our values onto our daughter throughout her childhood.

"I always knew that Sanjana would do something great in life as she has been referring to helping and influencing others since she was 10-years-old. Her starting something so massive at such a young age was a pleasant surprise for us. She has such a high level of understanding of some very critical components of life, and we feel so blessed and proud now that Sanjana is reaching more young minds and influencing them to make a big impact.

"The unique way that Sanjana thinks about her pathway to success is that making others successful or happy is automatically making her successful and happy. I truly believe that this is a very powerful viewpoint to look at the world. Sanjana fulfills her dreams and vision by fulfilling the dreams and vision of others.

"Success starts within you. You really have to know yourself and start to recognize and appreciate the power that you have inside of you. Know that the opportunities and the achievements that you can have are boundless. Your only restrictions are the ones that you put on yourself.

"Sometimes we as parents unknowingly, or to keep our children safe, try to induce our limiting beliefs on our children, and then we wonder why they are not successful. I encourage parents to stop programming your children with limiting thoughts and beliefs, and to encourage your children to explore various aspects and learn with free will. Once you have an understanding and agreement, then you can truly support their vision and goals so that they can soar up in the sky with nothing holding them back."

Amit Ambegaonkar

Sanjana's father

"Follow your dreams. You will accomplish great things and inspire others."
Leroy Blugh, Defensive line Coach for the Ottawa REDBLACKS Football Club

Chapter 3:
I AM A CRUSADER
Name: Kehkashan Basu - **Age:** 17
Hometown: Toronto, Ontario

"The young do not know enough to be prudent, and therefore they attempt the impossible – and achieve it, generation after generation."
Pearl S. Buck

MY DREAM

When I was very young, I became deeply moved upon seeing a photo of a bird that had died after eating plastic. I could not believe that a small piece of litter could be so destructive on a living creature. I wanted to do something to help the environment, but I did not know what, so I did what every child does when confronted with a confusing matter: I talked to my parents. They revealed to me that my birthday – the fifth of June – is World Environment Day, and in that moment I felt preordained to be an eco-warrior.

Just before my eighth birthday, I attended a lecture by explorer and environmentalist, Robert Swan, the only person to walk to both the North and South Poles. I was very inspired by his passion and his words: "The greatest threat to our planet is the belief that someone else will save it". I decided to start my own journey and began by planting my first tree on my eighth birthday with a monetary gift I received. That was my first green action, and I have not looked back since.

At 17-years-old I am the founder and president of the Green Hope Foundation, a youth sustainability organization that engages, educates, and empowers young people globally. What started with a handful of friends now has over 1,000 members working in ten countries, from Canada to the Middle East to the Indian subcontinent. I am also the Youth Ambassador of the World Future Council, a Climate Reality Leader, a United Nations (UN) Human Rights Champion, former Global Coordinator for the UN Environment Programme's (UNEP) Major Groups for Children and Youth, and a Child Ambassador for the UN Sustainable Developmental Goals.

I am also honoured and privileged to be the recipient of the 2015 Non-Resident Indian of the Year Award, the 2015 International Diana Award, the 2016 International Children's Peace Prize, the 2017 Turner Prize for Social Change, and the 2017 National Energy Globe Award. In my role as the voice of future generations, I have spoken at over 75 international conferences, travelling to several countries to emphasize my message of peace, gender equality, and the rights to education and sustainability. I also wrote a book called *Tree of Hope* about a young girl greening the desert, which was launched at the UN Children's Summit in New York in 2015.

My dream is to ensure that every person on this planet and future generations can inherit a clean, green, and sustainable planet in the same manner that we inherited from our forefathers. Our world is living on borrowed time. The global population has crossed seven billion, and at the current rate of consumption and wastage, we will need three "Earths" to sustain and feed the human population by the year 2050. Our planet is at the edge of a precipice: ice caps are melting, sea levels are rising, forests are turning into deserts, and yet our energy-hungry economies continue to add millions of tonnes of carbon dioxide into the atmosphere every day. My vision is to change this and ensure that a balance is achieved between society, the environment, and economic progress.

MY SUPERPOWER IS MY SELF-BELIEF

People have been against my efforts since I created the Green Hope Foundation when

I was 12-years-old. Almost immediately I became a victim of cyber-bullying from a person in my school: I was threatened with violence and stalked because the person was jealous of the work I was doing. It was a harrowing experience. One day I decided to speak out publicly against the threat, and I took to social media highlighting what I was going through. This really worked and made me realize that all bullies are cowards and take advantage of the fact that victims cower down and almost never speak out in public. I have since spoken about it on television and in print media to encourage other children facing similar issues to face up to their bullies.

Many adults used to put up barriers because of my age. They were very cynical about the fact that a 12-year-old ran a sustainability organization, and they did not take me seriously until confronted with my work.

I have become mentally stronger and learned to look adversity in the face and come out victorious. When I was 12, I was elected as the Global Coordinator for UNEP's Major Group for Children and Youth, making me the youngest person ever and the only minor to hold this position. This was a vindication of my belief that young people can take on positions of responsibility. I completed my term successfully, enhancing youth engagement tremendously and thus silencing all detractors, proving that age is just a number.

Speaking in public comes naturally to me and enables me to convey my message seamlessly to my audience, and my social media skills have improved as I regularly engage hundreds of young people through different websites. I still face the challenge of a lack of funding because, as a student, I need corporate support to conduct workshops and environmental campaigns, or to travel to and speak at conferences; however, I somehow manage support and have never had to curtail events or campaigns.

MY VOICE MATTERS

When I began my journey nine years ago I never imagined that I would be where I am today. I started off on my own with only one ambition: to make a difference, however small that might be. Along the way, several hundred people joined hands with me and now I am leading a movement on a global scale. I have been able to carry my message to over 25 countries across all the continents and create youth networks that are making a difference within their own communities. I am really proud of the scale of my impact, and I am glad that it continues to grow every day.

A lot of members at the Green Hope Foundation, especially those who are below 10-years-old, have told me that they try to follow my lead. They are convinced that it is possible to do well in their studies and, at the same time, work for the environment. I believe that every child has the potential to be a changemaker, and if I am able to inspire others to follow my lead and create a peaceful and sustainable world then I am putting my strengths to good use.

I value peace the most. It is the single most important criteria that can be a solution to all our woes. Peace brings us all together, and it teaches us to respect and thrive in the diversity of humanity. In order to achieve sustainability we must first achieve peace. Peace and education are interrelated, and one cannot be achieved without the other.

MY HEROES

I am deeply inspired by Mother Teresa. I have visited her institution, Missionaries of Charity, in Kolkata, India several times and worked with the orphans and street children who find shelter there. Her selflessness and passion to carry on with single-minded focus despite all odds have inspired me whenever I am confronted with challenges.

My parents have been my greatest support and have helped me stay grounded at all times. They gave me the confidence to live my dream and take up challenges without fear of failure. They told me that if I was honest, committed, and really believed in what I was doing then I should pursue my dreams wholeheartedly. They taught me to never take shortcuts and to work hard at achieving my goals. I owe my work ethic to their guidance. I am very privileged to have such wonderfully supportive and understanding parents.

MY ADVICE TO YOUTH

Believe in yourself for each one of you has the potential to be a changemaker. We are the last generation that has the opportunity to save our planet, so go out and make a difference. It is very important for youth to have the opportunity to speak for themselves. There are millions of children, especially girls, who do not have this right. This must change, and it is up to us young people.

To Adults

Remember that you were once children. Never underestimate the potential of a child. Rather, be open-minded and respect children based on their capabilities and latent talent.

"Kehkashan has always been very perceptive and caring. I realized her passion for the environment when she wanted to plant a tree on her eighth birthday. Thereafter, she went around the neighbourhood encouraging people to recycle, stop using plastic, and to reduce wastage. These were early signs that she was indeed very concerned about the environment, and I encouraged her to be confident and to not be afraid of failure.

"As Kehkashan's work became global and she started conducting workshops on various aspects of sustainability, she needed a chaperone as she was a minor, and I was more than happy to oblige. I took her to different UN conferences, and I became involved in civil society caucuses, particularly with relation to women's rights. I am also deeply engaged with her Green Hope Foundation, and serve as its director.

"Kehkashan is now a global youth icon, and her work is recognized internationally. Even though she is only 17, she is treated with respect and acknowledged as an expert. Every day she receives mail from youth from different countries wanting to join her cause. I am really proud of the global impact her work is having."

Swati Basu
Kehkashan's mother

"As a society, we value leadership, but we do not teach it well to the younger generation. Leading is in behaviour, not title, and the more younger children have that chance to lead and learn, the more of an opportunity they will have to grow and become courageous, passionate, and authentic human beings."

Shelly Elsliger, influencer
President and Founder of Linked Express

Chapter 4:

I AM A GUARDIAN

Name: Aura Chapdelaine

Age: 17

Hometown: Barrie, Ontario

"If you ever think about giving up, remember why you held on for so long."
Hayley Williams

MY DREAM

I have participated in most school activities since I was a young girl, and I have been a leader to my friends and the students in both my elementary school and high school. Many of my peers have come to me for help, perhaps because I am so outgoing and outspoken, and I continue to be baffled by some of their concerns. For example, some approached me during high school with the belief that they could not create change on their own because they were not on the Student Council, which I am a part of. The more I listened to these students, the more I realized that youth don't believe that one person can make a difference. I am a firm believer that this is untrue: everyone has the tools they need to achieve the goals they never saw possible. My biggest dream is to inspire today's youth to find their voice and speak up for themselves and their generation, and to teach them how to make a difference in their schools, communities and around the world.

MY SUPERPOWER IS UNLEASHING INNER VOICES

I am currently writing a book entitled *Take the Lead: 7 Easy Ways to Unleash Your Inner Voice* that I hope to publish by the end of this year. I am writing it to help both youth and adults realize that they have the potential to create change for themselves, those around them, and even others across the globe.

Step 1 is arguably the hardest step to achieve: building your confidence. When I was in grade eight, my confidence was very low as I delved into a really depressive state. I was so overwhelmed with school events, extracurricular activities, personal activities, and family issues that I forgot to look after someone really important: me. I worked hard to maintain my average of 92%, and after school I either had Student Council meetings, swimming, racquetball, dance, or sessions at the gym. From the moment I woke up until the moment I went to sleep, I was so busy!

I also found myself in a very awkward position: several of my friends were also depressed and naturally I wanted to help them, but I felt like I couldn't because I didn't feel like myself. Then my teacher presented the idea of a music camp to my class. I really wanted to go, but unfortunately I only had half of the money required, and that was from a monetary gift I received for Christmas. I spoke to my teacher about my predicament, and for reasons I am still unsure of, my teacher allowed me to go, even though I could not raise the remaining funds.

That camp was a miraculous transformation for me. There were so many different people playing so many different instruments at different skill levels that I had no fear of being judged by anyone. I discovered my passion for composing music – my "spark", if you will – and I learned that in order to build your confidence you have to find areas of interest that motivate you.

The next steps are a lot easier once you've built your confidence: become a better leader by helping people realize their value and worth; take time to focus on yourself so you don't burn out from too many commitments; learn to network to understand the importance of communicating through voice and body language; find your passion by creating a vision board about your goals; understand that it's okay to fail; and speak up.

MY VOICE MATTERS

Many people live life in fear and unhappiness. They know that something is wrong in their lives or the lives of others, but they are afraid to speak up in case a negative consequence befalls them. By teaching youth to speak up, I can help eliminate this fear, and people will be free to speak up in school, the community, and even on a national and global scale. The world as we know it could be a very different place. All it takes is one person to start the ripple effect of a movement and make all the difference. We are all worthy of being loved, happy, successful, and, of course, listened to.

MY HEROES

My friends are my heroes because of their ability to stand up when they've been knocked down, and smile and learn when they make mistakes instead of being hard on themselves. They inspire me to improve myself whenever I mess up.

Tony Robbins is also one of my heroes. In 2017 my mom discovered his Youth Leadership Program online, and my application was accepted just in time for his three-and-a-half day event "Unleash the Power Within" in New Jersey. This event was life-changing: it focused on personal growth and development, and it helped me break through my limitations and take control of my life through its emphasis on empowering youth to be leaders in the future.

MY ADVICE TO YOUTH

If you don't take risks you'll end up feeling nothing but regret. If you don't put yourself out there you will stay stuck in a maze that you created, and you will constantly get lost while searching for a way out. Sometimes the way out is just being able to say something.

To Adults

The more you force children to do something the less they want to do it. Let children explore their own ideas, and they will come to you for help when they want or need it. Sometimes stepping back means watching children fall first, but that doesn't mean you're doing a bad job. Communication is key.

"Things didn't come easy in my youth, but my life changes after I was exposed to *Think and Grow Rich* by Napoleon Hill. Inside its pages I saw my other self, and I was transformed with hope and a vision for a future I could create. Next, I listened to Tony Robbins' *Personal Power*, and I began my journey of service and personal growth to become an impactful leader.

"However, I still struggled! Even though I invested my time with others, I didn't feel worthy of the rewards that came my way from my efforts, so I pushed those rewards away. The result was a pattern of poverty through most of my adult life: I was making people millionaires while having a hard time feeding my own family.

"I persisted through it all, and eventually created an online platform called Angel-HillTV where I now help thousands of people build passive income using their passions and gifts online. Then, in 2016, something incredible happened: Tony Robbins – *the* Tony Robbins himself! – saw what I was doing through my work, and invited me to attend his 'Date with Destiny' event in Florida as his guest, along with my top three social media fans. After the event, I received a repeat invite to his 'Unleash the Power Within' event in New Jersey. It was at these events that I learned how to see and value my worth, and really create the impact I desired most. Day by day, my self-worth strengthens, and now I get to build *true* wealth in the process of service, and I teach others to do the same.

"Aura was greatly impacted by my experience and by Tony Robbins. We both truly recognized that we have the power to make a big difference, and we are continually working at realizing our potential. My daughter is my biggest hero and inspiration in life. She shows me balance in the world, and she inspires me to have more impact because I see how her messages of leadership impact others daily. Never before have I met a person so committed to creating her desired future. She boldly takes action with everything she puts her mind to, and she's forever in service to others. If everyone took a page from her book, this planet would surely be the best world we could dream it to be.

"We all have ways we can make our own mark. I am so proud that Aura and all the young leaders just like her in the world are finding their voices. These will be the true visionaries and creators of change and impact. I hope these stories inspire other youth to become leaders and let their inner heroes shine!"

Angel Hill
Aura's Mother

"Today's superhero kids deserve an education that's tailored to suit them. Freedom to learn. Freedom to grow. Freedom to be themselves. That's the true gift micro-schools offer today's kids."

Mara Linaberger, influencer, Ed.D., Author: *The Micro-School Builders Handbook* and *HELP! My Child Hates School*. Founder of Mindful Technology Consultants

Chapter 5:
I AM A VOICE FOR THE UNHEARD

Name: Sarah Chisholm - **Age:** 18
Hometown: Fort McMurray, Alberta

"I think women are scared of feeling powerful and strong and brave sometimes. There's nothing wrong with being afraid. It's not the absence of fear, it's overcoming it and sometimes you just have to blast through and have faith."
Emma Watson

MY DREAM

My dream is to create a mental health program that focuses on coping mechanisms, resilience, and self-esteem for people who have a mental illness, while also providing support for their families. I want to ensure that everyone suffering with mental illness across Canada is getting the proper care they need, and I want to be a voice for those who otherwise go unheard.

I've been an advocate for mental health awareness since I was 9-years-old. My mom sat on the Canadian Mental Health Association's board in Fort McMurray, and I often sat in on their meetings as they were right before my figure skating lessons. My mom was very passionate, and I learned a lot.

I had a very hard time coping, especially right after my high school graduation because a lot of my friends left town. In October 2017 I moved to Winnipeg, Manitoba, and I isolated myself from my friends and family. I felt so helpless and alone. I didn't know that I had such a strong support system that wanted to help me because I just couldn't get out of that dark place. I began seeing a therapist to learn coping mechanisms, and I was able to build up my resilience. Now I am able to open up about my experiences, and I know that I can use my experiences to help others going through similar things.

MY SUPERPOWER IS PERFORMING

I have been acting and modelling since I was young, and being onstage has helped me feel confident and has strengthened my public speaking. I entered a Miss Teenage Alberta contest three years ago, and I selected mental health as my platform. After winning the title of "Miss Teenage West Central Alberta 2016", I went to the Miss Teenage Canada Nationals in Toronto. I have spoken at different events in my town because of this, and I was given the chance to speak at Go Girls, which is a day for preteens to participate in workshops to build their self-esteem and try out different hobbies, like dance and photography.

MY VOICE MATTERS

I can change the world if I can put together a mental health program for those with mental illness, while simultaneously educating people on how to help those with mental illness. I've already started writing curriculum and making visual poetry pieces with my best friend.

MY HEROES

My mom is a super mom who has sacrificed so much to be able to be my number one fan. My family and I joke that she is my "momager". She has driven me to so many places, like to Western Canada Fashion Week in Edmonton, fundraisers, bridal shows, and photoshoots. My dad is also quite the hero because he has shown so much dedication to our family and works hard to be able to help me finance my dreams. My parents' teamwork and dedication to help me achieve my goals has inspired me a lot, and they have been the most crucial part of my support system.

I also look up to my high school teachers, Anastasia Uhlmann and Tammy Bradshaw. They facilitated the Student Council and Sexuality and Gender Acceptance clubs in my school, both of which I was part of, and they supported me in class and in extra-curricular activities.

I also consider Ashley Graham a hero of mine. When I first tried to model I fell short of my dreams – literally, I was too short! Ashley Graham, however, inspired me because she shows that shape and size don't matter. She is a plus-size model who has strived in the beauty industry and has given some amazing talks about self-love and confidence. She's truly a modern-day icon.

The owner of Bells and Bows Bridal, Angeline McDonald, whom I met while doing the Miss Teenage Alberta pageant, told me all about the volunteer work she does with her two service dogs, Cisco and Kobe. She is so selfless: she is involved with search and rescues, she aids her service dogs in the work that they do, and she helps girls find the perfect dresses to help them shine, whether it's onstage, a graduation, wedding, or any other special event. She helped me a lot while I was prepping for pageant season, and she has a way of making you feel like a million dollars.

Lastly, I was able to stay focused on my dream because of one of my dear friends who is passionate about helping others and who I worked with to put together a mental health presentation while we were Student Council presidents.

MY ADVICE TO YOUTH

My dad once told me that I grew up in a place called "Consequence World", and every action I took had a consequence, either positive or negative. I try to create a domino effect of positivity through positive actions. I urge youth to do the same: realize your self-worth, and shift your energy to attract positive experiences and people who respect your worth.

To Adults

Fill the young people in your life with so much positive self-esteem that nothing in the world can poke holes in the way they view themselves.

"Sarah is an enthusiastic student, motivated by a genuine desire to learn and understand. She is very keen on political participation, and I have told her I will vote for her even if she joins a party I would otherwise not support!

"What I find most notable about Sarah is her spirited involvement in many different causes, and her commitment to bettering the world she lives in. She's gone out of her way to make others feel comfortable and supported when they are unsure of their own abilities. I have seen this both in class and as a part of our Student Council, but she has also been involved in the larger community, particularly in projects surrounding positive body image and mental health in young people. The project that I have worked most closely with Sarah on is the development of our school's SAGA group, a support and information group for sexual and gender minority students and their allies. Sarah was one of the founding members, as she had observed the struggles that some minority students had in trying to fit in and deal with the harsh judgments of their peers. She is an advocate for those who feel they have little voice.

"It has been my pleasure to work with Sarah throughout her high school career."

Anastasia L. Uhlmann
Sarah's teacher

"We all want the best for our youth, that's without question. What *is* questionable though is why we keep doing things the same way they've always been done – prioritizing the same things, teaching the same lessons, trying to fit everyone into the same box instead of showing them how to create their own. Mediocrity is like a disease, and instead of curing it we're trapped in a cycle of promoting it, even celebrating it. Then we wonder why youth and adults alike keep falling well short of their true potential. It's time we raised the bar, not just on what we do, but on who we are."

Cory Chadwick, influencer
Founder of The Personal Greatness Project

Chapter 6:
I AM A UNIVERSAL SERVANT
Name: Gus Dallal - **Age:** 11
Hometown: King City, Ontario

"But those who hope in the LORD will renew their strength.
They will soar on wings like eagles; they will run and not grow weary,
they will walk and not be faint."
Isaiah 40:31 (NIV)

MY DREAM
I like to be funny and help people who need it most. When I started learning about poverty, it made me want to see world peace and the end of world hunger. It isn't fair that some people have a lot and some people have so little, so my dream is to see a world that helps everyone who needs it.

MY SUPERPOWER IS MY TAO HANDS TRANSMISSION
My mom has been going to Master Sha's Healing Centre in Toronto since 2016, and one day I decided to tag along out of curiosity. My mom has a chronic sickness that she often used to go to the hospital for, but I noticed that she didn't have so much pain when she went to the Centre, and I wanted to know more about it. I asked Master Vernier, one of

the teachers at the Centre, if I could join too. I have since learned about Tao Hands, a special transmission of positive light that helps people transform blocks in their bodies and minds.

I've used my Tao Hands to help lots of people maintain their health and happiness. One time my friend had a seizure, and I used my Tao Hands to help her body calm down until the ambulance arrived. She was okay in the end, and it made me feel happy to know that I was able to help. Another time my dad had a concussion and had headaches afterwards. I used my Tao Hands to offer him blessings to make his head feel better. I even used my Tao Hands to send a blessing to a dying plant in Lebanon. When I did, the plant had more energy and became healthy again.

I love going to the Centre, and I always feel better whenever I go. The teachers care about others so much, and want to help everyone they meet.

MY VOICE MATTERS

I am focused on finding my inner peace because that is the only way I can help others. I used to get angry when someone teased me or insulted me, but since I started going to the Centre I have learned to love myself, so I am not bothered by that kind of negativity anymore. Not only that, I try to transform that negativity. I have learned that a lot of mean kids aren't mean because they enjoy hurting others. They're kids who are hurting on the inside. They need help because something is wrong at home or at school, and all they need is a listening ear, so I don't judge them anymore. Some can still be mean, but others whom I have given my time to have actually become a lot kinder. If I can stop kids from bullying on the playground, then I will have stopped kids from growing up to be adults who bully in the workplace, or even in war.

MY HEROES

My heroes are Master Sha, Master Vernier, Master Sher, and Master Francisco. They are all teachers at the Centre who unconditionally love and serve every living thing. They never complain about anything negative in their lives, and their positivity runs 24/7! They have started me on the road to be a Universal Servant, and I am so thankful for everything they have taught me. Master Vernier specifically has also taught me to believe in myself and find my inner peace.

Master Sha is amazing! He's a special teacher and healer who helps people around the world by teaching them how to heal with the power of their souls. He's also offered transmissions like my Tao Hands to thousands of sick people and it has helped them.

Lastly, I look up to Terry Fox because he believed in himself even when other people didn't. He was so brave to run across Canada with one leg to raise money for cancer, and in the end he changed the world by doing it! I think of what it was like for him when he did that, and it makes me realize that we all have the power inside of us to change the world. We can become real-life superheroes!

MY ADVICE TO YOUTH

Stay strong and never let others put you down. You all have a special skill to help the world!

To Adults

Be amazing like my parents and support your children.

"As many mothers can relate to, my family has had financial and emotional challenges. I also suffer from painful migraines and ulcerative colitis, a condition in which ulcers develop in my intestines. In times of stress or anger, my migraines and ulcerative colitis flare-ups would become so painful that I would have to go to the hospital, but ever since Gus discovered the Tao Hands transmission my pain has been miraculously controlled. Somehow his love and compassion can overwhelm my pain, and I can rest easily instead of rushing to the hospital.

"Gus is an old soul with a big heart, and I have seen the positive changes he has created through his teachings from his Master Teachers. One such change is how he manages his anger. Instead of having an outburst or locking himself in his room, he chants, which calms him and allows for better communication. I try to help him stay focused any way I can, like finding time to chant or meditate, even if it's on the way to school and we play meditation music like 'Love, Peace and Harmony' in the car. I am so proud of Gus, and as the old saying goes: 'This little light of mine, I'm gonna let it shine!'"

Rola Issa Dallal
Gus's mother

Chapter 7:
I AM IN CHARGE OF MY OWN FATE

Name: Genevieve De Wys - **Age:** 12

Hometown: Kingston, Ontario

"Keep your thoughts positive because your thoughts become your words. Keep your words positive because your words become your behaviour. Keep your behaviour positive because your behaviour becomes your habits. Keep your habits positive because your habits become your values. Keep your values positive because your values become your destiny."

Mahatma Gandhi

MY DREAM

My ultimate dream is to make a difference in the world. I care about a lot of different issues, and sometimes caring can be my kryptonite. Sometimes I care too much about what people think of me, but I know that if I give into those fears then I will never reach my dream. My destiny cannot be reached unless I believe in myself and keep myself uplifted.

MY SUPERPOWER IS DREAMING

One of my dreams is to become an Olympic speed skater. I began skating at 3-years-old, and when I was seven I started figure skating. Whenever I came off the rink, I always told my mom that my favourite part was going fast. That led me to pursue speed skating, and I got 8th place out of all of Canada for long track speed skating!

Another dream of mine is to use my dual citizenship and travel to the U.S. to address issues such as gun violence, racism, police brutality, and Islamophobia. I am bothered that one person has the power to change these things, but decides not to. We all deserve to live peacefully.

Finally, I would like to be the first female Prime Minister of Canada. I am currently the Student Body President at my school for grades seven and eight, and I have been able to express my opinions and create change. I value honesty, and I want to create awareness for a variety of issues on a national scale, particularly for clean water and global peace.

MY VOICE MATTERS

I enjoy challenges, and whether I am in the Olympics, in the U.S. as a public speaker, or the Prime Minister of Canada, I would use my voice to speak for equality for all.

MY HEROES

My hero is Olympic speed skater, Clara Hughes. When I feel like I am having a bad day or that I am exhausted, I think of her story and everything she overcame to achieve greatness. She was depressed and abused by her coach, but she still went onto the Olympics. When I think of problems, they seem petty in comparison, and she gives me confidence and the ability to work hard to achieve my own goals.

MY ADVICE TO YOUTH

If you set your mind to something, don't let it go. If you have a passion you should pursue it.

To Adults

Give youth more independence because we need to learn from our own mistakes so we can become stronger.

"When I first started coaching Genevieve five years ago, she expressed her dream of being a top speed skater, which then led to her Olympic dreams. I always taught her to focus on smaller, more obtainable goals, as those will eventually lead her to achieve her greatest goals. More importantly, I told her that success only feels good after you have learned the disappointment of defeat.

"Fast forward to today, and I am proud of the young lady she is becoming. We have made an amazing connection, which has led me to being one of her positive role models. She even refers to me as her 'big sister', and I refer to her as my 'little sister'.

"Even though Genevieve may be 'just a kid' to many, her voice is still valid and can have just as much of an impact as an adult's voice – maybe even more so!"

Hayley Roberts
Genevieve's coach

"I started my first business when I was 17 years old. You are never too young or old to start anything or make a difference on this planet. All you need is to develop the qualities of tolerance, faith and unwavering determination, then you will be equipped with the necessary inner tools to being of great service to this planet."
Coach Nick Pereira (Nakula Das), Entrepreneur, Coach, Yogi

Chapter 8:

I AM STRONG

Name: Casey DeMerchant - **Age:** 14
Hometown: Harvey, New Brunswick

"The happiest people don't have the best of everything; they just make the best of everything."
Anonymous

MY DREAM

When I was 8-years-old, I started having extreme foot pain that was diagnosed as one thing and then another. As the years went on, I also started experiencing swelling, fatigue, and immune system problems. I was too stubborn to let those issues get the best of me, especially because I loved playing basketball and I refused to give it up! I went to bed with ice packs to relieve the pain, and just kept going with everything I loved. Eventually I started getting rashes, and issues popped up in my blood work that landed me in the IWK Health Centre in Halifax, the closest children's hospital to us, where I was diagnosed with juvenile arthritis. I was getting a bit better with treatment, but my mom couldn't shake the feeling that something was still wrong. Years prior her sister and brother-in-law had gone through a lot of the same issues, and they were ultimately diagnosed with Lyme disease, an inflammatory infection caused by bacteria. My mom thought there was a chance that I might have the same thing, but to get a proper diagnosis I had to have testing done through the U.S. That's what my aunt and uncle had to do because Canadian testing didn't help them. In January 2016, I not only tested positive for Lyme disease in the U.S., my result was so positive that it was classified as a positive result through the Center for Disease Control, which does not happen often! Since then I have had to make regular trips to New York to receive treatment.

My journey has helped me discover my dream: to help kids with Lyme disease in Canada realize how strong they are, and to let them know that they are not alone in their struggles. I hope that one day Canadians who suffer with Lyme disease will be able to get tested easily and treated correctly without having to leave their country.

MY SUPERPOWER IS MY POSITIVE ATTITUDE

I'm not going to lie: having a positive attitude while having Lyme disease is not always easy. There are days when I suffer extreme physical pain and discomfort, and I either feel frustrated that no one understands what I'm going through, or I feel angry, thinking that I'm the only one dealing with this disease, which I know I'm not. I've had to train my brain a lot over the years to keep a positive attitude. I try to keep a smile on my face, and even just forcing it sometimes makes real feelings of happiness shine through! I automatically start feeling better when I smile, and I've noticed that having a smile on my face makes other people around me happy too. I've learned that everything isn't always going to go my way or be easy, so if I want to get better, I have to be responsible for that, and the first thing is to change my mindset. It's true what they say – mind over matter!

MY VOICE MATTERS

I've never had a problem with people knowing my story because I feel like it's hard for people to understand your challenges without knowing what's really going on. If hearing my story can help someone else in any way, I'd rather have it out there in the open.

Lyme disease is very difficult to get diagnosed in Canada because Canada does not recognize "chronic" Lyme disease. Unless you are in the small minority of people who actually contract Lyme disease from a tick bite and develop a typical bull's-eye rash, then chances are that you will never be treated for Lyme disease in Canada – for now, anyway! I am going to change that!

MY HEROES

My hero is my mom. She has Lyme disease as well, and even though we have completely different symptoms, she knows what I'm going through. I admire how strong and brave she is – and how plain amazing she is!

I am also extremely thankful for Dr. Maureen McShane, my doctor in Plattsburgh, New York. I would not be where I am today without her help and encouragement.

MY ADVICE TO YOUTH

Never stop believing in yourself – you can surprise yourself sometimes!

To Adults

Kids are capable of many great things. Never hold them back from realizing that.

"The first word that comes to mind about what it's like to have Lyme disease is *'frustration'*. This journey has been a roller coaster! Casey and I went from doctor to doctor for Casey's ailments, ultimately going to the U.S. where she was finally correctly diagnosed. Dr. McShane expressed the concern that Casey got Lyme disease from me during pregnancy, and I was advised to be tested due to my own health concerns, things I just dealt with because doctors could never explain them. I initially said no due to costs, but as my symptoms got worse I decided to take the test and – surprise! – I was positive!

"While I love this country and aspects of its healthcare system, Canadian standards on Lyme disease need to be updated in a *major* way. People sick with this disease should not have to travel out of the country to get medical treatment – all along the way paying out of their own pockets. It is also challenging to have this chronic disease and have it treated as if it was not a real problem. It *is* a real problem, and with any problem that arises, awareness is key.

"In May 2016, Casey and I attended a demonstration at the New Brunswick Legislative Building in Fredericton for Lyme Disease Awareness Month. When I saw how many local people were affected and how many people were drawn to Casey, I knew how important it was for her to be an advocate.

"A year later I did a write-up for Lyme Disease Awareness Month on Facebook, and it spread so far, with many people sharing it and people contacting me afterwards for more information. I knew it was important to share Casey's story. People always take notice of kids who are going through something challenging, so they can be some of the best spokespeople! I've never met a coach, teacher, or anyone who knows Casey who doesn't tell me what a great kid she is. I am so incredibly proud of her. Not all children would have faced this disease the way that she has. It's a pretty special feeling to know that your child carries such strength."

Tammy DeMerchant
Casey's mother

"You are perfectly imperfect just the way you are. You are a gift, and your purpose is to selflessly share yourself with the world. To constantly be curious about who you are and who you are becoming. To find a means to share your learnings, your truths, your feelings, whatever they may be, with the others around you through the things that you love to do most. Thank you for being you."

Nicholas Theodorou, influencer
Photographer

Chapter 9:
I AM A PHOTOGRAPHER
Name: Leah Denbok - **Age:** 18
Hometown: Collingwood, Ontario

"If you judge people, you have no time to love them."
Saint Teresa

MY DREAM

When I was 12-years-old I took an interest in photography, but I soon felt like quitting because I didn't believe I was any good. My dad felt differently, and after some online searching he came across Joel Sartore, a photographer for *National Geographic*. He looked at my work and loved it! Soon afterwards he became my mentor, and when I was 14 he encouraged me to focus on portraiture since he believed this was my strength. Almost immediately I began photographing seniors in nursing homes, but I soon ran into problems with getting consent. Again, my dad came to the rescue: he came across the work of British photographer, Lee Jeffries, and suggested that, like Jeffries, I take photographs of people experiencing homelessness. Within a week I was in Toronto photographing this group of people, and I saw how little hope there is for so many of them.

At the same time I came to realize that homelessness is something that can happen to anyone. One man named Chris, for example, told us that he became homeless after suffering an emotional breakdown when his child and wife tragically died. After I began to meet and learn the stories of these people I became motivated to help them.

Through my work I have been trying to accomplish two goals: humanizing people experiencing homelessness, and shining a spotlight on the plight of homelessness. If these goals are achieved, then hopefully the general public will be moved to help these unfortunate people, and I will be able to reach my ultimate goal: to help end homelessness in the world.

MY SUPERPOWER IS PHOTOGRAPHY

I developed my skills as a portrait photographer in order to be able to get a good portrait on the street – sometimes in harsh conditions – in a five-to-ten minute time span. I also developed my relational skills to be able to interact with people experiencing homelessness, and I acquired the ability to empathize with them. I am pleased that through my photographs I have already been able to change some people's views and opinions about people experiencing homelessness and homelessness itself.

Unfortunately, sometimes I receive hate mail accusing me of exploiting those I photograph. It was disconcerting at first. However, Joel Sartore has instructed me to ignore such people. After all, I am making a difference in changing the general public's perception of people experiencing homelessness, and I have been able to raise thousands of dollars to help these people.

MY VOICE MATTERS

Notice how I do not say "homeless people". I prefer, whenever possible, to say "people experiencing homelessness". These people should not be defined by their unfortunate circumstances.

I am proud to have received numerous messages from people around the world telling me that my book *Nowhere to Call Home: Photographs and Stories of the Homeless, Volume One*, published in 2017, has inspired them to help those experiencing homelessness. I am also proud that, with the sale of this book, I have been able to raise money for homeless shelters.

MY HEROES

My hero is Saint Teresa (formerly Mother Teresa). I admire her because of the love, kindness, sympathy, and tenderness she showed to all people, and for the simplistic way she lived her life. Her seemingly boundless love for the poorest and most abandoned in society is very inspiring and won her the Nobel Peace Prize.

My other heroes are Joel Sartore and my parents. Joel has mentored me for four years, and when I first showed him my photographs of people experiencing homelessness he told me "it took my work to a whole new level". My mother has been incredibly helpful with regard to transportation, funds, and organization, and my dad is my manager and he accompanies me on all of my photoshoots.

MY ADVICE

To both youth and adults, I say: Never judge people you see on the streets. You don't know their stories unless you ask, and by doing so you just might learn a little bit about yourself.

To parents specifically, my advice is this: Help children to realize their potential. If you don't, it may never be realized. They need your encouragement and support.

"Leah's work has been influenced by my life because I was homeless as a child of three. I was found wandering the crowded streets of Kolkata, India, and Saint Teresa took me into her orphanage and raised me for two years before I moved to Canada with a new family. I am the first and possibly only child to be adopted to Canada from that orphanage.

"My story has given Leah a greater sensitivity to people experiencing homelessness, but I was nevertheless surprised when she first told me of her desire to take photographs of this less fortunate group of people. Then she said something to me that made me realize her great empathy: 'We are all just a pay cheque or two away from being homeless ourselves.' She truly understood the issue of homelessness at such a young age, and she never demeaned these people by referring to them simply as 'the homeless', but as 'people experiencing homelessness'.

"At just 13-years-old she began to be mentored by *National Geographic* photographer, Joel Sartore. Almost immediately after he began working with her he sent an email to my husband saying, 'If Leah sticks with it she is well on her way to becoming not just a good photographer, but a great photographer. And I'm not kidding.'

"I agree with Joel Sartore. For four years I have watched Leah give a voice to the voiceless and help others the way Saint Teresa helped me. I am happy to be able to assist in any way, such as the production of Leah's next photography books, exhibitions, and upcoming interviews for such media as CBC, BBC, CTV, WE Day, and *Chatelaine* magazine. Leah's vision has already impacted the world and will continue to do so by changing the perspectives of people to not have the 'them and us' mentality, but become aware of how many people around the world are impacted by homelessness.

"Like Leah, we can all help change the world by treating everyone we come across with dignity. I challenge all of us to leave this world a better place than when we were born."

Sara Denbok
Leah's mother

"Leah's work submerges you in another world. From what you read to what you see. She engages our curiosity and leaves us wanting more."

Matte Black
Founder of Heroes in Black and Leah's Supporter

Chapter 10:
I AM A YOUTH ADVOCATE

Name: Faith Dickinson - **Age:** 15
Hometown: Peterborough, Ontario

"Carry out a random act of kindness, with no expectation of reward, safe in the knowledge that one day someone might do the same for you."
Princess Diana

MY DREAM

I am only in high school, but I try to do whatever I can to better the lives of others: I volunteer at different events and masses at my church, as well as its Vacation Bible Schools in the summer. I am a Youth Ambassador for the Peterborough United Way; I hold food drives every year to support the Kawartha Food Share; I host a blood donor clinic every fall for Canadian Blood Services; and I have participated in several campaigns for Me to We.

My proudest accomplishment, however, is Cuddles for Cancer. When I was 9-years-old, my Aunt Lyndi was diagnosed with breast cancer, and I made her a fleece tie blanket. She loved it because she said her chemotherapy treatments made her very cold. I knew that I wanted to help other cancer patients feel warm, comfortable, and – above all – loved, so I created Cuddles for Cancer. What I thought would be just a summer project to help local cancer patients has turned into something so much bigger than I ever imagined! I have made an impact on so many people, and if everyone else did the same, just imagine how amazing the world could be! Everyone needs to be given the opportunity to soar!

MY SUPERPOWER IS MAKING BLANKETS

Starting a business with the word "cuddles" in it at the age of nine was pretty challenging – everyone just thought I was being cute! Once the cute factor wore off, I had to learn everything there was to know about owning and operating a business as quickly as possible. I had to create a budget, learn how to market my organization, fundraise, find sponsors, manage finances through a business account, and more.

As my business grew I became bullied in elementary school for all the attention I received. It was a *really* difficult time for me, but it never stopped me from pursuing my dream.

My successes, of course, totally overshadow any challenges that I've faced, and they pale in comparison to the challenges of those whom I donate my Cuddle blankets to. They're not just for cancer patients, but for Canadian veterans too. Whenever I give blankets to cancer patients, they are very touched that someone cares; that someone made them something that provides warmth, comfort, and love during one of the most difficult times in their lives. Veterans are moved that someone young shows that our generation will never forget the sacrifices they made so that we can enjoy the freedoms we do today.

Each blanket takes me roughly an hour-and-a-half to make, and each blanket has a story. A lot of cancer patients and veterans cry when they are given a Cuddle blanket. Those moments are very humbling for me. They show me that a simple gesture can mean the world to others, and that Cuddle blankets help make the world a better place.

MY VOICE MATTERS

Since creating Cuddles for Cancer six years ago I have made over 3,500 Cuddle blankets that have been sent to over 22 countries, including the U.S., England, France, Germany,

Brazil, Latvia, Australia, Iraq, Kuwait, Poland, Ukraine, Afghanistan, Zimbabwe, and Egypt.

Creating Cuddle blankets, as well as advertising them on social media, garnered international awareness. Four years ago I introduced Make a Difference Day to my local community. It is a day of awareness in the U.S. in which millions of people unite in a common mission to improve the lives of others. Right now we engage in community efforts like donating to food banks, but I hope Make a Difference Day (the fourth Saturday in October) will one day be recognized as a national day of community service – that would be a huge legacy to leave behind!

In 2015 I was one of four girls across Canada to be recognized as an exceptional role model by the Barbie Be Super campaign, but last year was my busiest year so far. I was one of 20 youth from around the world to receive the Legacy Award, in honour of Princess Diana, in England, and I created my very first physical location for my charity in Lakefield, Ontario: the Cuddles for Cancer Drop-In Centre. During the Christmas season my family and I organized an event there called The True Meaning of Christmas, and it was a huge success that included families, schools, business, and churches. We partnered with the Yellow Ribbon Campaign and Treats for Troops to support Canadian soldiers and veterans, and we invited the community to donate items for 19 boxes that were sent to soldiers serving in Egypt, Latvia, Iraq, Poland, Kuwait, and Ukraine. We also created Cuddle blankets that were delivered to the Pediatric Unit on Christmas Eve, and we decorated gingerbread cookies that we gave to seniors in Lakefield Extendicare.

MY HEROES

My parents are my heroes because they have helped me on my journey every step of the way. In the beginning they helped me understand nightmares I had following my first visit to SickKids Hospital in Toronto when I was nine. The suffering I had seen discomforted me, and my parents talked to me about how that had manifested into bad dreams. They made sure that I was okay, and that I understood what cancer was and how the treatments and surgeries helped the patients.

My parents are both entrepreneurs as well, so they really helped in the growth of my business – and my mom even came up with the company name! They taught me the importance of balance, and they helped me turn my mistakes into learning opportunities.

For example, after I became overworked and overstressed organizing four to five fund-raisers a month, my parents taught me to pull back and only organize three to four large fundraisers per year. In this way, I still pursued my cause, but in a way that allowed me to have time for myself.

I've also had some great mentors like Christina Abbott, retired peacekeeping veteran, Bill Steedman, and MP Maryam Monsef. I met Christina Abbott four years ago through her agency, STRUTT Models, in Peterborough. I regularly attended her girl empowerment and eco-activism workshops for over a year, and then I signed up with STRUTT to do some acting and modelling. She nominated me for the Legacy Award and has helped me host media launches, press releases, and different events. She encourages me to be the best that I can be, and I respect her as a businesswoman, an activist, and a friend.

I gave Bill Steedman a Cuddle blanket many years ago, and he has since become a family friend. He invites me to events at the Legion and the Armoury, and he helps out at events like Treats for Troops. He tells me who is in need of a Cuddle blanket, and he has introduced me to his fellow peacekeepers. He presented me with a necklace that says, "This girl is protected by Vets." I still have it to this day! He also nominated me for the Sovereign Medal for Volunteers in April 2017, and I brought him with me to Ottawa where I accepted the award from Governor General David Johnston. Bill Steedman has taught me about the needs of our military and the injustices they face.

Maryam Monsef has shown me amazing support over the past two years, and she has given me a lot of opportunities. These include helping me launch Women's History Month in Ottawa in November 2017; allowing me to be on the Peterborough Youth Council, which discusses key issues affecting youth in our community; and arranging for me to meet Malala Yousafzai in April 2017, who is a hero of mine as well because she took her personal tragedy and turned it into something inspiring.

I admire Craig Kielburger and Pinball Clemons for the impact they have made on so many youths through their respective organizations, Me to We and the Pinball Clemons Foundation. Princess Diana is also my hero because she brought awareness to causes that, during her time, were not socially acceptable. She was the first celebrity to hold hands with an AIDS patient, and the first royal to visit a landmine site. I hope my legacy will be as fondly remembered.

Finally, I consider Stu Saunders a hero. He is the founder of Youth Leadership Camps Canada (YLCC), which began over 20 years ago with only 50 kids. Now he has over 1,000 kids every summer, and he has reached thousands of kids globally through public speaking, such as annual youth leadership conferences in Niagara Falls. I had been going to Stu's summer camps for years, but I didn't meet him until 2015 when my cousin learned that he was speaking at Trent University. He genuinely cares about kids and wants them to reach their potential.

MY ADVICE TO YOUTH

Having a positive attitude in the morning *can* make a huge difference in your daily outlook. Surround yourself with people who believe in you and your dream, thank your supporters, and find your balance to stay healthy in mind, body, and spirit. You are never too young to make a difference. Go for it – I believe in you!

To Adults

Never tell kids that their dreams are too big or too impossible to achieve. Encourage them, be there for them, and take an interest in their interests.

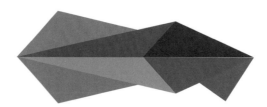

"Faith was nominated for The Diana Award and then went on to win the Legacy Award too. I met Faith when she arrived in May for the Legacy ceremony and I was blown away by her commitment to making a difference.

"Faith epitomises everything we believe at The Diana Award, that young people can change the world. Her commitment, selflessness and compassion are the qualities we celebrate and aim to instill in young people. What I admire most about Faith is how she quietly goes about, almost casually too, making a difference, without seeking applause or recognition. In my eyes, she is a true hero!

"Everyone has the potential to make a difference, everyone can be a hero if we pay close attention to the needs around. We can be that little bit more curious about the people around us and that is the first step to making a difference."

Tessy Ojo
Chief Executive of the Diana Award and Faith's Mentor

"We didn't know about Cuddles for Cancer when Faith first attended YLCC (Youth Leadership Camps Canada) four years ago. She eventually told her story to some of the camp staff, who then invited her to share her story during our 'motivational moments', where campers share with the others something that they are working on or have achieved.

"As Shaquille O'Neal once told me, 'good leaders don't look for credit for doing the right thing.' Faith is similar as she does not have an expectation for anything in return and created Cuddles for Cancer from her heart and out of compassion for others.

"Our motto at YLCC is 'Dream – Dare – Do'. If you can dream it, dare yourself to do it, and then *do it*. Challenge yourself because it makes you better. There are no extra people on this planet and we want you to challenge yourself because it makes you better, not more popular. Everyone is on this planet because they have a purpose and we want youth to discover their purpose and follow their dreams. Faith is an excellent example of taking an opportunity and creating something STU-pendous out of it."

Stu Saunders
Founder of YLCC and Faith's Mentor

Chapter 11:
I AM CARING

Name: Abby Fitzpatrick - **Age:** 10
Hometown: Kingston, Ontario

"You can do anything you put your mind to."
Benjamin Franklin

MY DREAM

I hope that one day everyone will put down their electronics and be closer to each other and to nature. I have noticed more and more people getting addicted to their devices, especially their phones. I have seen people on their phones while paying for their food at the grocery store – they don't even look at the cashier! How rude is that? Not only is it rude, it's not human, and not only is it not human, it's life-threatening. Did you know that bees are endangered now because of cell phone signals? Albert Einstein once said, "If the bee disappeared off the surface of the globe, then man would only have four years of life left. No more bees, no more pollination, no more plants, no more animals, no more man." That worries me. Our world is quickly becoming polluted by our actions. We are the ones ruining the only home that God gave us. We need to turn away from our phones and turn towards our fellow man!

MY SUPERPOWER IS MAKING PEOPLE SMILE

When people are bored or sad, most of them turn to their phones. They go on social media or play games or – for whatever reason – start watching endless cat videos! Sure, they become a little happier, but it's only for a short while, a distraction from the problems around them. But with a smile, I can help people solve their problems, not just forget about them.

When I was 5-years-old I was really shy, always hiding behind my mom whenever strangers came near, but I soon learned that the power of a smile goes a long way. When these strangers smiled at me, I felt happy, so I smiled back. So many brave people smile through their pain and made me feel stronger in my own situation. From there, whenever I saw my mom upset, I grabbed a tissue, gave it to her, and said, "It's going to be okay" with as big of a smile as I could muster.

That seemed to do the trick, and I've been making people smile ever since, especially at Roots and Wings, a community group that works towards encouraging racialized girls in Kingston to explore their diverse identities. I have joined lots of fun field trips with them, and I've learned about many things like cultural appropriation and cultural appreciation. Putting myself in someone else's shoes is one way I have made people smile at Roots and Wings. When people realize they are being understood and not just heard, it makes them feel valued.

MY VOICE MATTERS

I believe that a lot of unhappiness in the world today stems from people being attached to their electronics instead of to people. People feel a sense of instant happiness when they get a text or when someone likes a post on a social media page, and they text and post more to get that feeling again. Electronics can be like drugs, and I have been mindful to never let my personal devices rule my life. At school, instead of going on my phone during breaks like a lot of my peers do, I have volunteered as a lunch monitor for a grade one class, and I have joined the school choir. Lunch monitoring has helped me become more responsible, and performing at school events and assemblies with the choir has strengthened my singing voice and boosted my confidence. After school and on weekends I am at Roots and Wings, and every August I help my Nannie at a camp for special needs adults. Both Roots and Wings and camp have made me more empathetic and understanding of people with different needs and backgrounds.

There is so much to do and see in the world, and I would rather experience everything firsthand than through a screen on my phone. If I can convince people to do the same, then I am sure I can open the doors to some great experiences and friendships for them.

MY HEROES

My heroes are single parents who work hard to raise their children, especially my mom. She was in so many rough spots, but she still managed to keep a warm smile on her face. She also couldn't afford to get me a lot of electronics, and I think that's why I'm against their overuse as much as I am. My mom taught me the importance of love, kindness, and finding meaning in life through relationships with people and nature, not something shiny in the palm of my hand.

MY ADVICE TO YOUTH

Go outdoors and enjoy nature!
To Adults
Have more fun with your family and friends!

"Abby almost always has a smile on her face, which is amazing because she has gone through some very hard times. She was given a 50-50 chance to survive because she was born 25-weeks premature, and not only did she beat the odds, she is a very active kid, taking dance lessons and playing soccer. When she was 5-years-old, she and I moved away from my now ex-husband and life was hard for me. I was heartbroken with no money, and because of my immigration status at the time I could not work. But Abby used her superpower every day to put a smile on my face. She made me strong, and she continues to make other people strong, like through Roots and Wings. I have no doubt that Abby will use Roots and Wings to help her to soar into the world to help others!"

Tina Fitzpatrick
Abby's mother

Chapter 12:
I AM JOYFUL

Name: Michael Foster - **Age:** 17
Hometown: Alliston, Ontario

"You are only an attitude away from success."
John C. Maxwell

MY DREAM

Entering high school for the first time was very exciting. People were so kind to one another, and soon I became known as the tall guy who was always happy. I had an amazing time during my four years of high school, and I created memories that will last forever, but I also became really shocked by the amount of negativity surrounding everyone's lives. Kids were stressed out about assignments, exams, and their physical appearances. Some teens were even suffering from symptoms of depression because of circumstances with their families and friends. I'm a really positive person, so I couldn't believe how many people were so sad about life – and most about things that were temporary problems! I've had moments in my life when I've been sad, angry or self-conscious. I've also had tons of schoolwork and felt beaten down by some circumstance. However, as time passed I started to discover a rare piece of knowledge that most individuals around me had not obtained: how a positive mindset can influence your life. I refuse to look at life in the worst way possible whenever I am confronted with a problem. My vision is to change people's mindsets for the better, and to also show people the power of loving themselves and everything they have accomplished.

MY SUPERPOWER IS CHANGING PEOPLE'S MINDSETS

I decided that the first step towards reaching my vision was to become a Student Council member at my high school. In this position I am a voice for the student body, specifically representing grade 12. Through questionnaires, surveys, and our school news show on Instagram (which I produce with three of my best friends), I gain information from all students about what they would like to see in the school and plan accordingly, such as the South Simcoe Classic Basketball Game, a fun event that I created with one of my friends. In 2016 it boosted school spirit while also raising money for The Push for Change, a foundation that supports homeless youth. The following year the South Simcoe Classic helped raise funds for the Matthew's House Hospice's Helping Us Understand Grief (HUUG) program for youth mental health awareness.

I even travelled outside of my school to help my student body as the Student Senator. I was responsible for attending four meetings throughout the school year that included school senators from other schools in our board to discuss how to improve student needs.

I am a firm believer that accomplishing one's dreams is a step-by-step process. You first have to believe in yourself, then you have to have the will to try, and finally you have to act on your dreams. I accomplished a lot at my high school, and I managed to make a difference for my school community and the community at large. I was also able to focus on my own dreams through my internship at LMS Marketing and Management in the summer of 2017. I hope to be a part of sports marketing and event management so I can reach more youth and help them accomplish their dreams. The more successful people there are in the world, the more happy individuals there will be!

MY VOICE MATTERS

My superpower will make the world a better place because it will allow people to make them appreciate the things they have and may take for granted. Life is not always going to be easy – in fact, it seems to get harder as we grow older. The more independent we become, the more responsibilities we have, but our lives are what we make of them. If you have food in your belly, a roof over your head, clean water to drink, and clothes on your back, you are already on your way to success because so many people out there don't have those things. Be thankful for all of the positive things that you have in your life, and once you focus on that you will be happier and be able to help those who are not as fortunate.

MY HEROES

My heroes are my parents. My dad is one of the hardest working people I have ever known. Family friends have often remarked on how awed they are by what he has accomplished: he started off as a construction worker and is now one of the top project managers in his industry. My mom is one of the most compassionate people I have ever known. She once told me that I was an attitude away from success. I remember this piece of advice every day because it is the best advice I have ever been given. It is totally true: I have to remain positive in life because if I go off path for just a second I will regret it.

I am also thankful for my friends. I am an only child, and having such a great group of friends is like having a bunch of brothers and sisters. They are like my second family. I truly would not be where I am today without these special individuals.

MY ADVICE TO YOUTH

A man named Wylie Hudspeth once told me something his uncle had told him: "Wylie, we all get old and the majority of us will be sitting in a retirement home talking to others. Just make sure you're the person telling the stories, not listening to them."

You cannot lay back and let life come to you. You need to grab life by the steering wheel and drive yourself in the direction you want to go. Live your life to the fullest, find what makes you happy, and make sure that you have little or no regrets when you look back at your life. You only live once, so make it count.

To Adults

Keep kids on the right path in life so they are able to distinguish what is right and what is wrong. Be a good role model because we are a reflection of the important adults in our lives.

"When I was young my parents argued a lot. I dedicated most of my time trying to be the peacekeeper in my home, so I wasn't motivated to apply myself in school. I was not challenged to discover my true potential, and I gave up on myself. When I got older, I met my husband, Shaun, and his acceptance of who I was, without any judgment, deeply touched me. He awakened something buried inside me that I had kept quiet for so long. He empowered me to be the person that I am today – determined, focused, and driven – and together we created a television show called Future Prospects that showcases stories of inspiring youth. I founded the New Tecumseth Youth Advisory Committee to address youth concerns in our community.

"Our biggest accomplishment, however, was raising a son who refuses to settle on anything mediocre and instead strives for the life he wants to live.

"Every child needs to discover their self-worth and embrace their talents so that they can live happily. Each adult – especially parents – needs to step up to the plate and guide children. Don't be a friend to them; they already have friends their own age. Don't treat them like trophies or accessories; they're human beings. Most importantly, don't use social media or television to babysit them and raise them. They were not brought into this world by choice, so they need to be equipped with tools of life, and the best people to help them do this are the adults in their lives."

Joy Foster
Michael's mother

Chapter 13:
I AM A FAIRY-GODMOTHER-IN-TRAINING

Name: Kaitlyn Hantz - **Age:** 15
Hometown: Delhi, Ontario

"If you keep on believing the dream that you wish will come true."
Cinderella (*Cinderella*)

MY DREAM

When I was younger, my teacher, Tammy Vallieres, asked, "If you could have one wish in the world, what would it be?" Without a second thought I answered, "To be a fairy godmother and grant children's wishes."

That's all I want in the world right now: to fulfill my dream of being a fairy godmother. I know what you're thinking: "Fairy godmother? Like the one who sings the 'Bippity Boppity Boo' song in *Cinderella*?" My answer to you is: "Yes! Exactly!"

I'm sure many people wish that they could have a fairy godmother in their lives; someone who goes above and beyond to help them in their time of need, just like the one in *Cinderella*. Cinderella just didn't get to go to the ball, something she was really looking forward to – she got a gorgeous makeover, complete with a sparkling gown and a horse-drawn carriage to get her there! If I can be part of someone's happiness in any way like Cinderella's fairy godmother, whether it's providing a friendship, being a confidante, or fulfilling a dream, then I will be happy too.

MY SUPERPOWER IS BEING THERE FOR OTHERS

My life changed forever when I was 9-years-old. I woke up on August 4th, 2011 happy and healthy, but soon after I began to experience numbness in my neck and shoulders, which rapidly progressed down my spine. By noon I was rushed to the hospital, and by the end of the day I had transformed from a healthy, active girl who enjoyed dancing and figure skating, to being paralyzed from the neck down, unable to breathe on my own. I wasn't sick beforehand. I hadn't been in an accident. There were no symptoms indicating that something was wrong. I know it's hard to believe. The doctors performed every test possible to find a reason why this happened to me, and all they concluded was that I had contracted an autoimmune virus that attacked my spine.

I was diagnosed with Transverse Myelitis, a rare neurological disorder that causes an inflammation of the spinal cord, and my spinal cord was inflamed at the cervical section and went into the brain stem. The following nine months were spent in the hospital and rehabilitation centre where, after a lot of hard work and tears, I was able to come off the ventilator and breath on my own. I have regained all of my feeling in my body, though not a lot of movement.

A lot of amazing people in my life helped me with everything that I couldn't do on my own. I realized how I felt when others did things for me, most of the time without me even asking. That's when I decided that I wanted to be able to make others feel that way too. I can't give people makeovers or fancy rides the way the fairy godmother does in *Cinderella*, but I offer something else, something that I personally think is better: me. I am there for others when they need me, and that means more in the long run than any amount of money, fame, or fortune. I make people smile, and when I do that, those people pay my kindness forward and help others.

Most people just want to know that someone is there for them. I am, and I will always, be there to make people happy!

MY VOICE MATTERS

I used to say "poor me", but that never did anything for me. Instead of feeling sorry for myself, I decided to help others. I learned to be grateful for what I have because there will always be someone that is struggling more than me, and maybe I can help that person. Achieving my dream will not only make me a better person, it will help others become the best versions of themselves. If I can be part of making someone's dream come true, then that is all the joy that I will need in my life.

MY HEROES

My heroes are everyday people who work hard, are honest, and have integrity. Those people are my family and friends. Without them I would not be where I am today. They pick me up when I am down, they make me smile, and they love me unconditionally.

Tammy Vallieres is also one of my heroes because she brought a social and emotional wellness program into my elementary school called the Compassionate Crew. It provided monthly assemblies to help children learn virtues and values, and it also helped children awaken their inner heroes. With this program and with Tammy's help I was able to see a purpose in my life: to help others as much as I could, and to become a fairy godmother.

MY ADVICE TO YOUTH

Don't ever give up, no matter what life throws at you.

To Adults

Guide and support children with their dreams. Their dreams may not be yours, but they're something kids feel passionate about. *Please* don't ever tell kids they can't do it.

"On June 25th, 2013, I was riding my motorcycle on a beautiful sunny day. I felt so free, the wind rushing by me, and I was wearing my leather jacket with the logo of my favourite superhero, Superman, printed on the front.

"Then I suffered a hit-and-run motorcycle crash that left me paralyzed from the chest down. I was devastated. My injury not only impacted me physically, but also mentally. I lost my confidence completely. I knew then that I had two choices: either wallow in sadness over what happened to me, or regain my emotional strength, take back my life, and move forward. I chose the second option.

"I am the ninth of 12 people in the world – and the first Canadian – to receive a neural stem cell transplant. It was an experimental research study in Zurich, Switzerland in January 2014. I had high hopes of reversing my paralysis. Since the procedure, I have wanted to inspire others in the disabled community and give them hope – people like Kaitlyn.

"I met Kaitlyn in the fall of 2017 through a mutual friend. I immediately felt happy to be in her presence. She smiled like she did not have a care in the world, and she was very knowledgeable in an extensive variety of topics. We developed a deep friendship that is different from most others as we both understand life in a wheelchair.

"I admire Kaitlyn for her courage in sharing her story. I am moved and inspired that, through her circumstances, she discovered that happiness is not something you find; it is something you create. She is the epitome of courage and strength, and I am honoured to know her. She is like a little sister to me, and I am proud to call her my friend."

Lee Thibeault
Kaitlyn's friend

Chapter 14:

<u>I AM A SKATEBOARDER</u>

Name: Cole Hayward - **Age:** 15
Hometown: Princeton, Ontario

"If we want authenticity we have to initiate it. We will never know our full potential unless we push ourselves to find it. It's this self-discovery that inevitably takes us to the wildest places on earth."
Travis Rice

MY DREAM

I want to help find a cure for Amyotrophic Lateral Sclerosis (ALS, otherwise known as Lou Gehrig's disease).

I support ALS research because of the death of my father, who was only 29 when he passed from ALS. I was just 2-years-old at the time. In 2013 I decided that I could do something powerful about ALS: after seeing kids skateboarding during the London Walk for ALS, my friend and I created my own ALS fundraising event, which combined my love of skateboarding with my dream to help end ALS. It's called SK8 for ALS, and five years later it is still going strong!

MY SUPERPOWER IS SKATEBOARDING

For almost a year, my mom drove me to various places of business to round up prizes and sponsorship for my first event. Mitch Taylor, owner of Life of Leisure, and Matt Ashton, manager of The Boardshop London, donated prizes; Nick Hayward, my dad's brother and owner of The Fit Effect, sponsored our food table; and the Paris Optimist Club allowed us to use their skate park. I also contacted the ALS Society to notify them of what I was doing.

Our first SK8 for ALS competition was held in September 2014, the day after the London Walk for ALS. With over 50 attendees of all ages, SK8 for ALS was a huge success! Skateboarders competed on three features in the park in two age groups (15 and under, and 16 and older), and judges rated their performances and distributed prizes for first, second and third place in both age groups. We raised just shy of $1,200, and we decided that we would host another event the following year.

On September 19th, 2015, the second annual SK8 for ALS took place. With even more sponsors, donations, and community support, this event made headlines! We had coverage in the *Paris Star* and the *Brantford Expositor* the week before the event and again the week after. Even though it rained, we still had some die-hard skaters out to support and compete!

The event continued to grow, bring awareness, raise funds, and – best of all – bring the skateboarding community together in a friendly competition showing their support for everyone who has been touched by ALS. We have raised almost $5,000 so far for ALS Canada!

MY VOICE MATTERS

ALS is a debilitating disease. The muscles of the body break down to the point where people can't walk, talk, or eventually even breathe. Most people who suffer from ALS won't live past two to five years after diagnosis. It is important for me to raise as much money as I can to support ALS research so that I can help find a cure for ALS.

MY HEROES

In addition to skateboarding, I also love snowboarding, and professional snowboarders,

Darcy Sharpe and Mark McMorris, are my heroes. I admire them for doing what they love and never giving up. Mark McMorris specifically has had a lot of injuries that he was able to overcome, and he still pushes boundaries in the sport.

MY ADVICE TO YOUTH

Always try and make a difference. Never give up!

To Adults

Help others, and do good deeds!

"I was overcome with emotion when Cole told me he wanted to do something to honour his Dad, Jake Hayward. I also thought it was a unique and appropriate idea for him because of his passion for skateboarding. He had a tag line right away: 'Boarding for those who can't!'

"As we work together in this, Cole shows that you should never judge a book by its cover. Skateboarders have a lot of judgment on them: there is an assumption that bad things happen at the skate park, and that skateboarders are rowdy troublemakers. This is just not so. This skateboarding community – a group of young people – have come together and made a huge difference!

"Watching Cole's dedication to his cause has impacted my life greatly, and it continues to touch my heart. He is truly doing this in memory of his dad so other kids don't have to go through what he has been through."

Stephanie Hayward
Cole's mother

Chapter 15:
I AM EXCITED FOR THE FUTURE

Name: Zachary Hofer - Age: 13
Hometown: Barrie, Ontario

"Shoot for the moon. Even if you miss, you'll land among the stars."
Norman Vincent Peale

MY DREAM

I'm a pretty active kid: physical education is my favourite subject, and I love basketball, rock climbing, bouldering, and jumping on trampolines. I think it's important for kids to be active and to find things they enjoy doing because being active helps you stay healthy and happy. That's why I want to become a gym teacher. I want to teach kids about the importance of health, and I also want to be especially encouraging to those who are sick. When I was little I read a book about Annaleise Carr who swam across Lake Ontario to raise money for kids fighting cancer. Since then, I've been inspired to help kids feel better. I don't like seeing them upset or sick or struggling, and there are so many kids today who suffer from poor mental health. Three years ago I participated in a Terry Fox Run, and I decided to do something similar. My mom always said I could do anything I put my mind to – even though she first said no to my dream to run across Canada! – so now I am focusing on making kids happier!

MY SUPERPOWER IS MY ATHLETICISM

In 2017 I began living out my dream to go across Canada, spreading awareness about youth mental health. I trained for nine months, approached sponsors for support, and spoke to thousands of students in schools and at events to raise awareness for my journey and to tell kids to reach out to an adult if they were struggling mentally.

On August 13th, 2017, I set out on a 29-day journey from Barrie called Zach Makes Tracks. I walked, ran, and cycled to raise funds and awareness for the new Child and Youth Mental Health Unit at our local hospital, the Royal Victoria Regional Health Centre. My original goal was to raise $10,000, but after rallying my community, other towns, and even our nation's leaders, I have raised almost $110,000 – and it's still growing!

On September 10th, 2017 I arrived in Ottawa and walked onto Parliament Hill to the cheering of a very large crowd. I met with Prime Minister Justin Trudeau; former Minister of Health and Long Term Care, Eric Hoskins; Minister of Child and Youth Services, Michael Coteau; former Minister of Education, Mitzie Hunter; Premier Kathleen Wynne; and many more dignitaries to ask them to make youth mental health a priority in our country.

When I first told my mom that I wanted to help kids, I didn't realize that speaking in front of people would be involved. I really dislike public speaking – it makes me so anxious! In fact, people in Barrie know me as the "boy of few words"! But using my voice is the best way to raise awareness for youth mental health, so I had to start working hard to overcome my fear. My mom, my step-dad, Derek, and our Public Relations Expert, Sylvia, helped me feel more comfortable with speaking, and so did some friends who were radio announcers and TV personalities. They especially helped me with interviews and answering hard questions.

MY VOICE MATTERS

Like Ellen DeGeneres says: "Kindness can go a long way." Being kind to people will inspire them to be kind to others, and it just feels good. My mom and Derek told me just to speak from my heart because all of my answers are there.

I'm slowly getting better at public speaking, and I even talk about my fears and anxieties at schools I'm invited to speak at. My mom says that doing so shows other kids that they don't have to be the loudest person in a room to make a big difference. I've already impacted kids in my community: some have started their own fundraisers to help me by running bake sales and lemonade stands!

I've been on TV many times, and I even did a live interview with Wei Chen from CBC. I don't mind speaking one-on-one, and I was comfortable when I spoke with our Prime Minister. I wasn't afraid to say something wrong, but I was a bit intimidated because he was tall!

MY HEROES

I admire Terry Fox and Annaleise Carr for their bravery and initiative to help people, and I am lucky to have lots of heroes so close to me. During Zach Makes Tracks, Derek always motivated me, and my mom read me messages from people who were supporting me. This helped me to keep going when I wanted to quit.

My mom, Derek, Sylvia, the foundation at the Royal Victoria Regional Health Centre, and all my sponsors and supporters helped me find whatever I needed on my journey, and they also shared my story so that others knew what we were doing.

MY ADVICE TO YOUTH

Be persistent. If someone says 'no', just keep trying.

To Adults

Listen to your kids when they want to do something good.

"When Zach first told me his dream was to run across Canada like Terry Fox did so he could help kids, my initial response was 'NO!' That's right: I said 'no' to my child's dream. But Zach was persistent – for more than two years! Eventually one of his teachers asked me why I was saying 'no' to Zach's dream. Was it because I didn't think Zach was serious, despite talking about it for so long? Was it because, if he was serious, the whole undertaking would be exhausting? My reasons for saying 'no' paled in comparison to saying 'yes'. I realized that I *do* want a kid that sees that things need to change, who sees that people need more, who *wants* to make a difference. I wanted to be a 'yes' mom, so I said, 'YES!' And Zach Makes Tracks was born.

"Zach has always believed that we can all make a difference if we work together.

As early as age four, Zach made sure everyone felt okay, sitting with the child who had no partner, or inviting the shy child to join in play. His empathetic nature has only grown. Zach has been able to reach and motivate kids across Ontario in a way that adults can't: through his humility, honesty, struggles, and triumphs.

"Zach has seen me go through mental health issues. I have Major Depressive Disorder that goes in and out of remission, and my treatments include an almost four-hour daily drive to Toronto and back for weeks at a time. Zach told me that his dream was to make things better so that other kids don't have to grow up this way. Children are experiencing more and more difficulties with mental health issues, and we are quite far from having a perfect treatment system. Only one-in-five youth receives the treatment they need – that isn't good enough. You wouldn't wait a year to get treatment if your child broke a leg – why do we wait so long for mental health treatment? This is a global issue. We need to learn more and teach our kids better skills and tools to manage stress and anxiety. Let's get this sorted out *before* it becomes a life or death situation.

"I'd by lying if I said Zach didn't want to quit at some points. Sometimes it was as easy as adding a bag of jellybeans to his bicycle to keep him going. Sometimes we had to have long talks about being committed to this journey, and that he had to stretch outside his comfort zone and do a live interview, or speak with a big group of kids. We never pushed; we always made it so he was the one who agreed to do anything.

"We can't believe the support of our sponsors and our community. They all believed in a little boy who asked for help. Zach often says: 'Even if one kid reaches out for help, and even if we never knew, *all* of this would have been worth it.'"

Shelley Hofer
Zachary's mother

"I have held on to my childhood belief that we are capable of making great change for the betterment of all living beings when what inspires us comes from a pure belief and a deep inner knowing. "

Heather Haynes, influencer
Artist & Creator of the Wall of Courage

Chapter 16:
I AM POWERFUL

Name: Emma Howse - **Age:** 11
Hometown: Delhi, Ontario

"Be the change you wish to see in the world."
Mahatma Gandhi

MY DREAM

My dream is to be on Canada's Olympic Swim Team. I recognized this vision in my heart when I first began swimming with the Norfolk Hammerheads, a swim team in Simcoe, Ontario. With the help of my friends, I was able to become faster and move up through different groups. When I am chosen for Canada's Olympic Swim Team I will be so happy to have achieved something that I've wanted for so long – and I will walk with pep in my step!

MY SUPERPOWER IS SWIMMING

I'm a superhero, and when things get rough I use my superpower to swim my absolute hardest! That's how I got to Regionals: I trained and was able to compete with swimmers from Hamilton to Windsor! In February 2018 I made it to Festivals, the next level of competition after Regionals. I went to Ottawa to compete against other qualifying swimmers from across Ontario. I kept practicing and getting better and better, and now I am so proud of myself! I also watch past Olympic races to help me stay focused on my dream. Watching those swimmers helps me remember to work hard and push through, especially when faced with a tough challenge.

MY VOICE MATTERS

My parents, coaches, friends, and teachers tell me all the time that I am strong, that I can do anything, and I have come to believe those words. More importantly, I believe in myself. I want to show people that anything can be done if you put your mind to it, and that everything you want can be done with lots of hard work.

MY HEROES

I wouldn't be where I am today without my friends and family. They're important to me and have supported me every step of the way. I also look up to my former swimming coach, Maddie Heggie, because she always swims to the best of her ability, which encourages me to reach my dream.

MY ADVICE TO YOUTH

With lots of hard work and dedication, anything is possible! Just believe in yourself!
To Adults
Encourage children to find their passion and guide them towards their goals.

"I am an alumni swimmer from the Norfolk Hammerheads currently swimming for Campbell University in North Carolina. Frequently I'm told by young athletes that they dream of going to the Olympics. I always do everything I can to help them get better, but in the end it comes down to what they're willing to do. When I coached Emma she worked extremely hard at every practice, putting in 100% effort and doing everything she could to make herself better. She rarely missed practice, and she did exactly what was asked, even when it was challenging; like following specific breathing patterns, going deeper underwater after each push off the wall, and doing out-of-pool workouts such as running and squats. She also had a profound influence on her fellow teammates: by doing her best in practice, Emma challenged those around her to go faster in practice as well. Emma's personal successes at competitions motivated her teammates because, due to the competitive nature all athletes have and need, they wanted to feel the same sense of achievement. It's great to see how one person can impact so many others. She provides evidence that one person *can* make a difference."

Maddie Heggie
Emma's former swimming coach

Chapter 17:

I AM NOT AFRAID TO BE MYSELF

Name: Dexon Huyck - -**Age:** 6

Hometown: Napanee, Ontario

"Be who you are and say what you feel, because those who mind don't matter and those who matter don't mind."

Dr. Seuss

MY DREAM

I knew I was a girl when I was 2-years-old. I knew it in my heart, and I told others so they knew it, too. A year later I cut my hair to make it grow faster, and my mom and dad let me wear dresses. Maybe I wasn't born a girl, but that doesn't matter. What matters is that I know I'm a girl, and my mom, my dad, and my four brothers know it too, and when I grow up I want to be a mom and love my kids the way my family loves me.

MY SUPERPOWER IS BEING TRUE TO MYSELF

Some people say I'm different, but thanks to the people around me I have never felt different. When I was 4-years-old, my mom and dad took me to a big hospital called the Children's Hospital of Eastern Ontario (CHEO) in Ottawa, and the doctors said that my parents were doing the right thing in supporting me. My teacher supported me too: she let me wear princess dresses at school!

A few kids made fun of me at first – and on Anti-Bullying Week! I went to school wearing a dress, and I got teased. One girl said I was a boy, and I stood up for myself and told her that she was hurting my feelings. I stayed true to myself, and I wore a dress the next day – and the next day and the next! Kids at school started to accept me, and I made friends. The girl who hurt my feelings even came over to my house!

MY VOICE MATTERS

I want to show kids that it's okay to be you. The world will accept kids who feel different if we tell them it's okay to feel different.

MY HEROES

My hero is Jazz Jennings. I've seen her lots of times on YouTube. She is a girl like me, and she speaks out for people who are born one way and feel different on the inside. She also made the TransKids Purple Rainbow Foundation with her parents to help kids like me.

MY ADVICE TO YOUTH

Be who you are and not who others want you to be. My 94-year-old grandpa agrees!
To Adults
Let kids be who they are and love them no matter what!

"At a very early age Dexon identified with being a girl, and my initial thought was that this was just a phase. My husband and I soon discovered that it was not a phase, and that it was beyond an emotional attachment to stereotypical female toys, clothes, and behaviours. I was not familiar with what Dexon was experiencing, but I admired her courage to be herself from an early age. Our journey isn't always easy for my child or my family; however, we have had tremendous support from the community, school, and doctors.

"As parents, we need to let our children be who they are, and even though it is difficult, we need to steer away from forcing gender biases on them. Love is the greatest gift you can give and receive, and loving someone for who they are benefits everyone."

Monica Huyck
Dexon's mother

Chapter 18:

I AM AN ARTISTIC SCIENTIST

Name: Mushahid Khan - **Age:** 15

Hometown: Brampton, Ontario

"Strive always to excel in virtue and truth."

Prophet Muhammad (peace be upon him)

MY DREAM

Usually there is a great disparity between people who love the arts and people who love science. I am one who loves both and hopes to merge the two in my career choice to make the world a better place. I enjoy science, with a strong passion for quantum physics, and I also enjoy technology, while simultaneously dabbling in acting, filming, photography, and sketching. My dream is to develop full dive virtual reality. I've been interested in virtual reality since seeing a sci-fi television show called *Sword Art Online* where there was a headset that allowed the characters to enter a simulated world that felt real to them. I want to make those worlds a reality.

MY SUPERPOWER IS CREATIVE THINKING

I am a fast learner, skilled at math, science, technology, and the arts. I like using all of my skills together to create influential pieces, such as a recent project with Reel Youth, an organization that works with youth to create films about different issues in the community. In November 2017 the theme was homelessness, and I created a documentary with three others about a man named Ken who experienced homelessness in our community. All films from this project were aired on CBC National, and I am happy to share that we were also able to raise funds at the screening.

My brother, Ayaz, and I have been volunteering for as long as I can remember. The one organization that stands out in my memory and has been the most fun working with is Peace Tree International, which I have supported since the age of six. Ayaz and I organized a screening of the movie *Peace Tree Day* by Mitra Sen, founder of Peace Tree International. We even started our own NGO called Save the Earth Man (S.T.E.M.), which supports the environment through plantation drives. We approached the Department of Environmental Planning with our plan to give plants to people for free, and the Department donated young trees to us in support.

I am proud of my accomplishments, and I look forward to strengthening my skills in order to pursue my dream. I am currently satisfied with photography and filming, but I am planning to run a business someday, so I have to learn advanced techniques. I'm looking forward to intern with the film production company, In The Zone Media Production, as they are doing commendable work in the community. I'm also aspiring to start a photography and film company by applying for a youth business grant with guidance from the Brampton Economic Development Centre.

MY VOICE MATTERS

My documentary through Reel Youth was successful, and I decided to continue raising awareness for homelessness by fundraising and filming in February 2018 during the Coldest Night of the Year Run. The event raised over $100,000! I have been able to turn dreams into reality in little ways, and I am excited to create realities that will bring the dreams of many to life.

MY HEROES

My parents have been significantly influential. They encourage me to stay humble and to volunteer my time towards causes that would make the lives of others better. They also gave me the great advice to always stay true to my word. That has been ingrained in my brain.

My grandparents have taught me patience and positivity, and they taught me the message given by Islam to be mindful of neighbours, share your blessings to spread happiness, promote peace, and to be tolerant in the face of adversity.

Prophet Muhammad (peace be upon him) has influenced me since I was a child. My parents and grandparents told me stories about his life, and his actions have motivated me to try to tell the truth.

Lastly, I admire Albert Einstein. His work in physics was extraordinary, and we would not have a lot of the understanding we have today if it weren't for him.

MY ADVICE

To Youth

Self-doubt is your biggest enemy. Ignore it and keep working. When I believe in something and someone says I can't achieve my goal, I put in double the effort. For example, one of my high school teachers pushed me to take an applied course instead of academic, suggesting that I would not be able to perform at the higher level. I told my teacher to have faith in me and let the results be the guide, and if I could not showcase aptitude by the end of the term then I would take the applied course. Such an action did not need to be taken as I did very well at the academic level, and I am proud of it.

To Adults

Tell children how great they are. Science shows that children who are praised are more likely to accomplish great things in their lives as they grow older. When my mother praises me or my brother, we laugh it off, saying that she only does so because she is our mother; however, the fact is that her praise feels good, and we are motivated to excel.

"Mushahid has exhibited maturity and compassion from an early age. When he was only 6-years-old he accompanied his brother, Ayaz, and a group of friends to walk around the neighbourhood distributing saplings for plantation drives. A year later he and Ayaz voluntarily sang for the participants of an early morning yoga class where I volunteered as an assistant teacher. Most participants were seniors struggling with health conditions, and many were happy to see such young children, not only singing classic vocal bhajans (religious and spiritual songs), but also joining in yoga!

"As a mother, I am proud that my son is both logical and humane. I remember not too long ago a moment in Toronto when a man experiencing homelessness approached us on the way home from an event, and Mushahid was visibly upset that we did not have any cash on hand to give to him. We found another way to make amends by arranging donations for meals at a community kitchen.

"I am a firm believer that giving up is never an option; one must always find a way – create one, if necessary – to achieve a goal, big or small. Believe in yourself. If you don't, then why should others believe in you?"

Taranum Khan, Ph. D.
Mushahid's mother

Chapter 19:
I AM COMPASSIONATE

Name: Maya Kooner - **Age:** 12
Hometown: Vancouver, British Columbia

"Today you are You, that is truer than true. There is no one alive who is
Youer than You. "
Dr. Seuss

MY DREAM

I'd like to think I'm just a regular kid: I go to school, I have friends, and I play sports. Recently something happened that makes some people think I'm more than just a regular kid: I landed a role on *Lemony Snicket's A Series of Unfortunate Events* on Netflix.

This opportunity was so unexpected. I was so happy when I got the role, and I've been having a blast on set. More importantly, it has made me realize that if I gain publicity with this role, or any other future role, I can have a huge impact on kids and adults of all nationalities across the world, especially those suffering from mental illness.

I learned a lot about mental health through my mother because she works in healthcare. So many people in the world need help from mental illness – including kids!

– and yet there are not enough resources. Mental disorders are related to the brain, so my dream is to become a neurosurgeon.

MY SUPERPOWER IS GARDENING

My mom and I got involved in a community garden called the Riley Park Garden in the spring of 2017. Students from the agricultural program at the University of British Columbia work on the garden, and we learned a lot from them like digging, plowing, when to plant seeds, how to properly water the garden, and which crops to harvest and when. We grow vegetables and herbs, and then we harvest our growth and donate it to help feed the less fortunate at the Mount Pleasant Neighborhood House. Anyone in need is also free to take from the garden itself so that they can get fresh and healthy food to cook at home. The cool thing is that there are so many people that work on the garden, so I get to meet a lot of people, like Eddie, a 90-year-old man who started the garden over 20 years ago.

I believe working in the garden is a way to relieve everyday stress. Stress can be challenging to deal with, but I learned that I have options: I can either go home and do some mindless activity like lie in bed or play video games, or I can work in the garden and gain a sense of peacefulness. No other activity replaces how my mind feels after gardening. I am helping people in need through gardening, and I have learned that you don't just walk by a person in need. You have to help them. That is our duty.

MY VOICE MATTERS

In addition to gardening, I also love acting, and the one great thing about acting is that I can reach lots of people at once, especially through social media, or even through the characters I portray. One of my favourite shows is *Grey's Anatomy* because I love watching how the doctors work tirelessly to save people. They are non-judgmental towards every patient, just how I hope to be when I become a neurosurgeon.

MY HEROES

My heroes are my parents and brother. They have always been there for me and have supported me through everything. On production of *Lemony Snicket's A Series of Unfortunate Events* they come with me early in the morning and stay until late in the evening. I see other kids filming who are by themselves, and that makes me sad. Having my family there is very important to me.

So far my heroes have helped me achieve everything, but one day I will reach my goals on my own. I know I will because I am very committed to whatever I do, whether it's sports, acting, gardening, or schoolwork. I always try to do my best. Sometimes my best is all I can do. My heroes taught me that. They also posted the best advice on our fridge. It's the rules of ABC: be *A*uthentic, *B*elieve in yourself, and be *C*ompassionate.

MY ADVICE TO YOUTH

Never give up on what you want. I wanted to act, so I went for it full force! My mom got me an audition with Premiere at Walt Disney, and I got to meet kids from 13 different countries *and* I got to meet actors Miranda May, Lauren Taylor, Kayla Maisonet, and J.J. Totah! A memory that I will cherish for the rest of my life is when Lauren Taylor laughed at the joke: "Did you hear about the guy who got hit with a soda can? Good thing it was a *soft drink*!"

During my Walt Disney adventure I was told that if I got a callback from an agent or producer I was one of the lucky ones, and you know what? I got five! Plus I got signed on with Conneckt Creative Agency in Vancouver! Never give up pushing for what you want!

You also need to remember that making a positive difference is simple: it's about making the right choices every day. You don't need to change the whole world in a day or week. Ttake one step at a time by being an active person in your community and doing your best to help. You also need to make the right choices that are healthy for you: eat healthy, participate in sports, and stay away from drugs. Don't get peer pressured into doing something you don't want. It won't make your life any better. If you're really stuck, find a friend, teacher, or neighbour who you can talk to. Only you have the power to make your life better.

To Adults

Kids don't have it easy. There is a lot that goes on in the playground. There is a lot we have to deal with, but we just want someone to understand. That person can be a parent, teacher, or even a neighbour.

Us kids learn from you. If you are happy then we are happy. If you work, then most likely we will work. If you study, then so will we. I understand adults don't have it easy either, but together we can make it and get through any challenges because I believe if we love each other no matter what, the rest will fall in place.

"I know I may be biased, but I have always seen a glimmer in Maya's eyes, and her determination starting as a young infant has been exceptional. I remember when we visited San Francisco: Maya was only two and she refused to sit in her stroller, but rather pushed it up the hills of Alcatraz! I couldn't believe what I was witnessing! Now as a pre-teen, that determination has translated into her being totally dedicated to everything she decides to do. She completes her homework on time, memorizes scripts, *and* performs in front of 40 cameras at age 12 – I don't think I could do that!

"The amazing thing about Maya is that she has done so much already. She may change directions and find herself on a completely different path, and that is perfectly fine. I have created a safe space for her in our home, surrounded by her family who loves her the most, where she can learn that it's okay if sometimes things don't go her way, and she can embrace those experiences rather than be discouraged by them.

"I grew up in a generation of books, magazines, and encyclopedias, whereas today's kids are engulfed with social media like YouTube, Twitter, and Instagram. They can figure things out quicker and more efficiently than those of my generation. I always say use the system – don't fight it! Learn how to do this, and you will create a moment in time. Every child should be encouraged to experiment with their journey whatever that might be, but in a safe manner and with a sense of hope."

Sara Garcha
Maya's mother

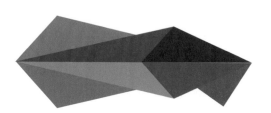

Chapter 20:
I AM IMAGINATIVE
Name: Mckenna Lumley - **Age:** 13
Hometown: Windsor, Ontario

"Every great dream begins with a dreamer. Always remember, you have within you the strength, the patience, and the passion to reach for the stars to change the world."
Harriet Tubman

MY DREAM

I want to find a cure for brain tumours.

I was diagnosed with a brain tumour when I was 4-years-old after I woke up early one morning vomiting and with pain in my neck. Upon being diagnosed, I was rushed to Children's Hospital in London, and I had two major surgeries in three days. Since then I have been tumour-free!

I know firsthand what brain tumours can do, not just for the person suffering from them, but to their families as well. I have seen how scary and sad brain tumours are for many people. As a survivor, I realize I am one of the lucky ones, and I want to do something to help those impacted by brain tumours.

MY SUPERPOWER IS MY IMAGINATION

My reality has been difficult at times, so I often get lost in my imagination. My imagination helped me through a lot of medical procedures, tests, and even brain surgery. I also had a back surgery that was especially difficult after I was diagnosed with scoliosis when I was 8-years-old. I had a spinal fusion to straighten my spine. A titanium system of rods and screws were attached to the curved part of my backbone, and then small pieces of bone were put over my spine. In time, the pieces will fuse with my spine. It was extremely painful, and I don't like to think about it. I prefer to look at where I am now, how great my posture is, and how physically strong I am!

Because of my experiences, I wrote a book called *The Secret Portal* about how people can use their imagination to help them through difficult situations. I got the idea after an MRI five years ago: I started daydreaming, and the next thing I knew I had created a fabulous land! I asked my mom to write everything down, and I have since turned that story into a book!

MY VOICE MATTERS

Can you imagine a world where no one suffered from brain tumours? The world would be a far less scary place! I have started making changes that will hopefully lead to such a world.

Since 2010 I have participated in the annual walk for the Brain Tumour Foundation of Canada, and over the past eight years our family and friends have raised over $120,000 to support brain tumour research. Each year my brother, Blake, and I create a team name that gets our family and friends excited about supporting us. We used to have a fairy theme because I absolutely love fairies, but last year we were known as Team 9¾: Witches and Wizards Against Brain Tumours because I am obsessed with *Harry Potter*!

In 2015 my friends and I started a business called Glitter Glam: Tattoos for a Cause at our school. For the past three years we have charged $2 to students during recesses and school festivals to create magical glitter tattoos on people's arms. We have raised over $3,000, and all of our money has been donated to the Brain Tumour Foundation of Canada.

In addition to raising money for brain tumour awareness and research, I also speak publicly about my experiences at different events, usually for Children's Hospital. During Brain Tumour Awareness Month (May), I take extra time to speak to as many classes as I can. Sharing my story raises awareness, but more importantly, it gives people hope.

MY HEROES

Meriel Reed, who is also featured in this book, is one of my heroes. We met at the Children's Health Foundation's Magical Winter Ball in 2015. She spoke and sang at the event, and I knew I had to meet her. When we met, it was as if we had known each other forever. We danced all night, and ever since I have considered her to be one of my best friends. She was one of the only people I wanted to see when I was in the hospital, and she knew just what to say and do. She also made me a beautiful heart pillow to comfort me – she is unbelievably talented!

I also admire activist Malala Yousafzai. She too was in a terrible situation, and after she escaped death she decided to make a difference in the world, like I am. She was shot in the head because of her views on girls' rights to education, and instead of being quiet and giving into fear, she became stronger, and is now one of the most influential people in the world. She encourages me to do something important with my life.

MY ADVICE TO YOUTH

Dream big, don't give up, and use your imagination!

To Adults

Support children. Sometimes their ideas are the ones that change the world.

"When Mckenna told me to write about a magical land she had visited during one of her MRIs, I didn't think much of it at first because she always created stories in her mind. However, she kept with it, and I gladly helped her every step of the way.

"Mckenna has always been an optimist, which is especially amazing and admirable because of the hardships she has been through. Sometimes I worry about how positive she is, as strange as that is to say. I worry that she puts on a brave face and may be hiding anger and stress under the surface. I think it's dangerous not to deal with your true feelings because mental issues could develop later on, but Mckenna is a fighter. She could have crumbled on more than one occasion, and I never would've blamed her. Whenever my own challenges are cluttering my mind, she refocuses me and brings me back to what's important in life. My daughter is my hero."

Karen Metcalfe
Mckenna's mother

Chapter 21:
I AM A GENIE

Name: Jax McMackin - **Age:** 12
Hometown: Truro, Nova Scotia

"I don't know how I'm going to live with myself if I don't stay true to what I believe."
Desmond Doss

MY DREAM

I like to think that I am a normal 12-year-old boy who loves the Boston Bruins and the Toronto Blue Jays and the Raptors, but I have something rare that makes people think I am not so normal, because they don't understand the way my mom and I do. I have dysautonomia, which means I am sick every day. Sometimes my heart beats way too fast and I can feel it in my chest; sometimes it beats too slow, which makes me feel dizzy. There are days when my body temperature is too hot, and other times when I feel like I am freezing. All of these symptoms often make my blood pressure abnormal.

Obviously I am not the only kid with some kind of illness. There are so many all over the world suffering from different diseases, and when I was 6-years-old I got to help one of them. I wanted to help my mom raise money for the Children's Wish Foundation for a boy who was very sick and wanted to go to Disney World to meet Harry Potter. I started a lemonade stand and in two days I raised $1,000! Everyone in town came to buy lemonade from me! I knew then what my vision was: to help people bring out the hero inside of them. Everyone is born to be kind, even if you have to go out your way to do something for someone, and it feels so good. I want to give people the feeling I felt when I helped this boy.

MY SUPERPOWER IS GRANTING WISHES

I have been sick since I was two or three, but I was only able to talk about it after the Children's Wish Foundation granted me a wish in September 2016. Before then I never wanted to talk about my illness because I didn't want to worry anyone, especially my friends at school who often asked where I was whenever I was absent because of a hospital visit. My wish seemed to give me power – like a superpower – to talk about my illness.

When I got to pick my wish, I was so excited that I didn't think about my next scan or blood work. It was a crazy feeling because I am sick every day with headaches and nausea, so to forget about all that for just a little while was so relieving. So many sick kids are not guaranteed to live, and tomorrow may not come. Sometimes sick kids like me just don't make plans. But to get a wish is like getting the greatest gift in the world: time.

I was so happy when I was granted my wish. I wanted to go to Pearl Harbour in Hawaii because I love history, and I knew right away who I was taking with me because they were the first to come and visit me every time I was in the hospital: my cousin, Sadie, and my Aunt Melissa. In Pearl Harbour we swam with sea turtles, learned to train dolphins, hiked Diamond Head (a volcano), visited the war memorial site, and met a 99-year-old Pearl Harbour survivor – I was so amazed just being able to shake his hand!

In 2017 I was asked by the Children's Wish Foundation to help grant a wish to a boy who was diagnosed with leukemia. His wish was to have a pool in his backyard to swim in with his family. I helped pack the UPS truck and deliver the Wish to the boy. It was the most amazing feeling ever to see all of my hard work go to making him smile so big, and I even created a team called Jax's Warriors that includes my friends to bring joy to sick kids! I'm like a genie granting wishes!

Shortly after, I was chosen by the Children's Wish Foundation to represent them in front of 100 Women Who Care, a non-profit organization of 100 women who vote on which charities to donate money to. It was intimidating at first because I was the only boy in the room, but I won $5,000 that went to the Children's Wish Foundation to help grant another Wish!

I never thought I could speak in front of hundreds of people, but I did. I never thought I would be able to grant other kids' wishes, but I have. I never thought I would be educating others and making people smile just by being kind, but I do. I am so proud of myself! I am proud that I have been able to help grant Wishes from all of my fundraising – I have raised over $10,000 for children just like me by hosting charity events like barbecues, selling old toys online, and from 50-50 draws I created. I have made people feel good by doing good.

MY VOICE MATTERS

People say I am inspiring, like how I am sick some days and still make it to hockey. It makes them not complain about the tiny things that go wrong in their day. Maybe I am inspiring, but I do not see myself that way. I think I am contagious with kindness! If I am kind to others then I expect that they will be kind also. Being kind is easier than being mean. When you smile, others around you want to smile. The best words to show kindness are "I love you". I love hearing those words right before I fall asleep, and I love saying those words too. Whether I say them or hear them, those words make me feel safe.

MY HEROES

My mom is my living hero. She is with me every day, helping me when I am sick and scared. She always knows how to make things work out, even when she has no idea what she is doing. She figures it out.

Buddington, a Therapeutic Clown at the IWK, is my hospital hero. He has been with me on my journey for as long as I can remember. He is the funniest, craziest, best clown friend ever! He has a magical way of always making me forget what is going on around me, and every time he has to leave, he never says goodbye, but "Take care, panda bear!" I love it when he says that! He is living proof that laughter is the best medicine.

My spirit heroes are Viola Desmond and Desmond Doss. Both of these people stood up for something they believed in, and both knew they could have died for their choices. Viola Desmond was a Canadian Black woman who challenged racial segregation after she was told to leave a white-people-only area in a theatre, and Desmond Doss was a U.S. Army Corporal who served as a combat medic in the Second World War. Viola Desmond will be the first Canadian woman to be featured on a Canadian banknote (the $10 bill), and Desmond Doss was the only Conscientious Objector to receive the Medal of Honor.

My friends are very important to me because they make the days at school much more fun. It gets hard to focus in class when I feel like the room is spinning and I want to throw up. My friends have helped me love school by treating me like they treat everyone else, and they have a lot of patience for me when they know I need help. They also help me catch up when I am in the hospital.

My gym teacher, Mr. Brian Hayden, always makes me feel good about myself. I am not a good basketball player, but I love basketball, so I am encouraged when he yells, "Great job, Jax!" or "Nice play, Jax!" He always asks if I took my medications and if I ate. He won't let me participate unless I have done those two things. Every school needs a teacher like Mr. Hayden.

My family supports me every day, which makes me feel stronger. They are the one group of people that will always be there to help me find ideas to fundraise, and they give their time to come out to charity events even when I know they are busy. They always tell me they love me, and they make me feel normal. Sadie is like my sister. She has been through everything with me, from blood work appointments to tests, and in school we play sports on the same teams. My Nanny and Pappa McMackin are there for me every single day too, even though they live in New Brunswick. I can call or visit anytime I want just to say, "I love you." They stayed in the hospital with me every day for months, and they still come down to visit when I am not feeling well, or to watch me play hockey. I love looking up from the rink and seeing my family cheering me on. My Uncle Ryan makes me feel good too by taking me fishing whenever I visit him, and even though he is in Newfoundland he always calls to tell me a joke.

MY ADVICE TO YOUTH

Wayne Gretzky once said, "You miss 100% of the shots you don't take." He is right:

if I don't take a chance then I will never know if I could have done something. Even though I am only 12, I can do so much, except I can't give blood. You have to be 17. Did you know that I could save three lives by donating just one time? My mom said I can't change this law. So, if you're 17, go donate! If not – or even if you are – know that every single one of you can be a hero. Heroism is inside all of us if we try very hard and don't give up on our dreams. If you can dream it then you can make it happen.

To Adults

If you're a parent, always say "I love you" to your kid at the end of the day.

"I remember the very moment I realized Jax was a very special child. He was only 3-years-old, sitting in a wheelchair because of all the medical lines and tubes he had in his little body, and I wheeled him into the playroom of the IWK Health Centre for a much needed break for us both. He wanted to be near the window, and when we arrived he noticed a boy sitting on his own and Jax said, "Mom, I need to get a book for the child sitting all alone." He disregarded his own circumstances to help someone else in need.

"At that moment I knew I was raising a hero, and it was no easy task. I needed to learn to accept the things I could not change and, boy, were there a lot! I needed to mourn the child who I had imagined I would be raising. I never imagined that I would be raising a sick child. Jax has gone through so many surgeries, scans, tests, and hospital stays. He battles every single day. Having a sick child on a daily basis is a unique and difficult challenge all on its own, but I also worked full-time as a police officer, which presented its own challenges. As time when on, I received a career-ending back injury, and then I became divorced. The world kept on spinning, and I knew we needed to keep spinning with it. Without Jax, though, I don't know how I could have. He was saving my life as much as I was saving his. Despite the pain he goes through, he wakes up every morning with a huge smile on his face, ready to start the day anew. He never complains about his illness, even when it completely derails his days and our plans.

"Three years after I wheeled him to that window in the IWK playroom, Jax told me he wanted to help raise money to grant a wish to a sick child. He was only six, but he came up with the idea of hosting a lemonade stand that also sold cookies to raise even more money. He raised $1,000 in two days, and has not stopped fundraising since.

"I have received so many incredible emails, cards, and letters thanking us for creating awareness about the Children's Wish Foundation and thanking me for raising a child who knows the true essence of what it means to put good out into the world. I am proud that Jax has taught me and so many others that how you make someone feel will last a lifetime.

"I know that God has big plans for my child, and that by fully supporting Jax, I am creating a wonderful, kind human being who will know the value of putting good out into the world. There is no *way* I would stop him!"

Lana McMackin
Jax's mother – and his biggest fan!

Chapter 22:
I AM FUNNY

Name: Harley Moon - **Age:** 8
Hometown: Napanee, Ontario

"The things that make me different are the things that make me ME."
Piglet (*Winnie-the-Pooh*)

MY DREAM

My dream is to help create a world without pain, and to help kids not be sick anymore.

I was born with Sturge-Weber Syndrome (SWS). I have a large birthmark on my face called a port-wine stain, and for as long as I can remember I've had seizures and glaucoma, an eye disease that I need check-ups for so I don't become blind. I see lots of doctors, I've tried lots of different medicines, and I've had over 100 different surgeries! My biggest surgery was in January 2012. It was called a hemispherectomy, and the sick part of my brain was taken out.

I don't like seeing doctors. I know they're trying to help me, but the tests and medicines sometimes hurt, not just me, but my older brother. He doesn't like seeing me go through what I do. He sometimes cries. I know he worries about me.

If my dream comes true, then I won't have to worry about being hurt anymore, and my family won't hurt either. If I can help me and my family, I will be so happy to help others!

MY SUPERPOWER IS TELLING JOKES

I love jokes, and telling them makes me feel stronger when I see my doctors. My appointments go a bit better after a good joke. My favourite joke is:

Knock, knock!

Who's there?

Sam.

Sam who?

Do you like green eggs and ham?

I told this to my glaucoma doctor when I met him for the first time, and he couldn't stop laughing!

MY VOICE MATTERS

The best way to reach my dream is to raise awareness, and my family and I have done lots of things to help people learn about SWS. Did you know that May is Sturge-Weber Awareness Month? Well, you do now! I just raised awareness!

Every May my family and I put up posters in different stores about SWS, and last May we had a baseball fundraiser to raise money for the Sturge-Weber Foundation and a surgery for me to remove a cyst from my brain. We had face painting, popcorn, snow cones, cotton candy, raffles and a baseball game! Between that and a spaghetti dinner fundraiser we raised almost $6,000!

I am also one of the Ambassadors for Easter Seals South East Ontario. For almost 100 years, Easter Seals has helped families buy expensive things like wheelchairs and ramps for kids with physical disabilities, and they run two summer camps for kids with physical disabilities called Camp Merrywood and Camp Woodeden. I've gone to different places around town and talked about how Easter Seals help my family. I even go on our local news station, CKWS, during Easter Seals Tribute Week every April!

MY HEROES

My hero is my brother, Gavyn. He goes to a lot of my appointments, and he always makes me laugh if I'm sad or scared – most of the time by letting me kick him! He also inspired me to ask for donations for my last two birthdays instead of presents because he did that for his birthdays. In 2016 we raised $300 for SickKids, and last year we raised $185 for the SPCA!

MY ADVICE TO YOUTH

Remember that adults in your life are trying to do what's best for you, even when it doesn't seem like it. Try not to give them a hard time.

To Adults

Keep being the heroes that children believe you are.

"The hardest thing for me to do for a long time was ask for help. I was very controlling when it came to Harley's needs, and I did not feel comfortable relinquishing any of that control, even to medical practitioners. I also felt regret and guilt because I was so caught up in all the medical complications and unknowns with Harley that I was hardly there for my eldest. Our journey has been eight years so far, and I still feel sometimes that I don't have any idea of what I am doing, but I have learned that there are hidden blessings in this world if I just quiet my mind and ask for help.

"Harley has had tremendous support over the years. Every challenge our family has faced has been overcome by love from family, friends, doctors, and members of our community. They have empowered us when we have felt drained, and they have strengthened us to conquer every trial without hesitation. Through them I have found more strength to better help my daughter.

"Because of her young age, I don't know if Harley's dream is just vocalized thoughts or something she is determined to achieve. Harley often randomly says that she wants to help others, even if the conversation has nothing to do with that topic at that time. I think it is her innocence talking right now, but if what she says is more than just words, I will guide her in any way I can. I hope Harley never loses the will to want to help others because actions, rather than words, speak volumes."

Candice Roberts
Harley's mother

Chapter 23:

I AM A PEACEKEEPER

Name: Elijah and Nephtali Neplaz

Age: 12 and 10, respectively

Hometown: Toronto, Ontario

"In a gentle way, you can shake the world."
Mahatma Gandhi

MY DREAM

Elijah

I love animals, and it breaks my heart to see them mistreated or hurt. I remember once seeing a bird in a park near my house that was dying because its neck was twisted, and I felt powerless because there was nothing I could do to help it. I knew it was going to die. When I was in grade six I did a project on animal cruelty, specifically killing animals for fashion desires. Seeing animals in pain and hearing about injustice towards animals in the world makes me sad, but these stories have also motivated me to help animals. That's why when I grow up I want to be a veterinarian.

Nephtali

I have a deep love for music thanks to my mother who has sung to me since I was born.

I want to be a singer when I grow up so I can bring hope and love into people's lives the way my mother brought hope and love into my life through her singing.

MY SUPERPOWER IS ADAPTING

Elijah

A lot of animals learn to adapt in order to survive. That means when presented with a challenge or a different situation, they have to change themselves in order to survive. Some animals migrate to warmer areas during colder seasons, while others hibernate. Other animals camouflage to escape predators. Like some of the animals we love, we have learned to adapt to our surroundings so we can overcome any challenge.

Elijah

The first big challenge I faced was when I was just 5-years-old. We used to live in the French Caribbean where we enjoyed nice weather, beaches, and lots of fun in the ocean. Then we moved to Canada because my parents wanted my sister and I to have more opportunities to achieve our dreams in the future. It was cold and snowy, and the only word I knew how to say in English was "hello". It was hard, but I caught on pretty quickly, and now I can speak fluent English.

My biggest challenge nowadays is making a bridge between two worlds: the world that I live in with my family that focuses on love, positivity and compassion, and the world that society is creating that focuses a lot on the dark. Most news stories are about what is wrong in the world rather than what is good; song lyrics are often negative and explicit; and many of my peers are more invested in their phones than with each other. I feel different sometimes, and being different isn't always easy to deal with on a daily basis. It's hard to keep doing the right thing when you're the only one doing it. Sometimes I feel the temptation to follow the crowd. Thankfully my parents have taught my sister and I different meditative practices and chants that help me remember my core values and adapt to situations around me. This will help me as a vet because I know there are lots of challenges to get there – like first getting my university degree – and then all the different cases I'll work on.

Nephtali

When I told my dad that I wanted to be a singer, he did some online research and came across the Ben Heppner Vocal Music Academy, a school in Scarborough that mixes music into all subjects. The idea was so exciting at first, but then it became really nerve-racking. I was very hesitant to leave the school I was already in. It was French Immersion, which I was very comfortable with because French is my first language, and I didn't want to leave all the friends I made. I was faced with a tough choice: stay where it was comfortable, or try something totally different. I chose the second option, and since joining the Ben Heppner Vocal Academy, I was chosen as one of the lead roles in their production of *Sound of Music*. I landed a spot in the choir as a soprano and we competed in the Toronto Kiwanis Music Festival; and I won a talent show! I am well on my way to reaching my dream!

MY VOICE MATTERS

You can put a price on a laptop, and if it breaks you can just buy a new one. You can't put a price on a life. If a life has ended, sadly, you cannot buy another. Life is precious, whether a human life or an animal life or even a plant life. Words are a very powerful thing, and our voices are and will continue to be used to spread love.

We are part of a band called Jia Chang Vibe, and we regularly help people release emotional blockages like stress and anger through our meditation music. We are always touched when someone tells us that our music has transformed them. In the summer of 2017, for example, the mayor of North Bay listened to our music during the North Bay Festival, and he loved our music so much that he asked the event manager to book us for another show the next day!

Love makes people happier and healthier. We see how love works every day. The smallest thing – smiling at someone, greeting someone, or holding the door open – can change people's days – and even lives – for the better.

MY HEROES

Our heroes are Haile Selassie I and Mahatma Gandhi. Haile Selassie I was the emperor of Ethiopia for 40 years, but for five years he was forced into exile after Italy invaded his country. When he was allowed to return, he encouraged citizens not to take revenge on the Italians remaining in Ethiopia, and he began to modernize his country with different changes to society, schools, and the government. He showed true love, forgiveness, and compassion by not engaging in war with the people who wronged him.

We also admire Mahatma Gandhi because he stopped a war using loving words, not fists or swords.

Lastly, our parents are our heroes. They uprooted their lives from the Caribbean to come to Canada to better our futures, and they inspire us to be creative.

MY ADVICE TO YOUTH
Learn to be flexible so you can face any challenge, and find someone to talk to whenever you feel alone.
To Adults
Sometimes it's hard for kids to keep doing the right thing because they do not want to suffer isolation. Please help them during these times. Give them love and affection. They will continue to make the right choice.

"Having a world living in love, peace, and harmony is my biggest goal because there is too much suffering in the world today. Helping one another is not 'trendy' anymore, and growing up mentally, spiritually, and physically healthy is very hard. The truly upsetting thing about this reality is that it is everyone's reality because we are all connected. We are all one. We must look after one another, and more often than not we choose not to.

"My wife and I try to show our children how kindness, forgiveness, and love can transform a family, a neighbourhood, and more. We love spending time together as a family, and my wife and I talk regularly with our children about what makes them vibrate inside; what emotions and passions stir them. As pre-teens, Elijah and Nephtali are musically gifted, and have persevered through a huge move from the French Caribbean to Canada. They also follow their hearts, even if their belief does not follow general opinion. They're not rushing into adulthood, and they enjoy being young. My wife and I could not be prouder of them. We support them as we support anyone who wants to make the world a better place: through creativity, hard work, and faith."

Gilles Neplaz
Father to Elijah and Nephtali

Chapter 24:
I AM MORE THAN A DIAGNOSIS
Name: Mack O'Keefe - **Age:** 18
Hometown: Burlington, ON

"Look into the darkness, and it will oppress and consume you. However, if you're will-ing to look into the light, know that even the tiniest shimmer can pierce the darkness."
Mack O'Keefe

MY DREAM

I was diagnosed with autism when I was 3-years-old. While I watched my siblings play and swim in the pool, I often worked with a therapist in a quiet part of our house. As a kid, I didn't quite understand or care about why I needed extra help because I didn't understand how I was different. As I got a little bit older, I could see that there were differences: I had difficulty being imaginative, and I was late developing language. I began to have a better understanding of how all the work I was doing through my inten-sive therapy program was helping me, and the work was fun too because my siblings, friends, and cousins were often involved in working with me on my social skills. I now appreciate the work that I did, and the work that my family and team of consultants and therapists did. My dream is to live my best life – to contribute and have a full social and professional life. This is a dream that will be realized.

MY SUPERPOWER IS INSPIRING OTHERS

I inspire and help other children with autism and their families. I am 18-years-old; I have had many lead roles in school and community plays, such as Armand Beauxhomme in *Once on This Island*; and I have been accepted to all of my top university choices. I am also a lifeguard; I have a black belt in taekwondo; I have my driver's license; and I am going to Kenya with my school this summer to aid struggling communities. When other parents hear about how much I have accomplished it makes them raise their expectations for their children with autism. Inspiring and empowering other people is what I get my greatest joy from.

MY VOICE MATTERS

Being positive and willing to tell my story and share my experiences is important. I have an important voice and a perspective that should be shared.

MY HEROES

I have a lot of heroes. There are too many names to list here, but I hope they know that not a day goes by when I'm not thankful for all the effort they have put into raising me, especially my family and my developmental consultant, Am Badwall. Along with members of my community, teachers, and mentors, they have all been patient with me, and have worked together to make sure I can succeed.

MY ADVICE

Look into the darkness, and it will oppress and consume you. However, if you're willing to look into the light, know that even the tiniest shimmer can pierce the darkness. God has a plan for all of us, but it's up to us to find out what that plan is and stick with it. Don't give up or throw in the towel; people look up to you, love you, and care about you.

"I met Mack when he was 3-years-old. He was a happy little boy with the brightest spirit; however, there were clear challenges that were evident upon meeting and assessing Mack's development: underdeveloped speech and language; restricted and ritualistic patterns of behaviour; and a deficit in social understanding and appropriate social interactions for his age.

"With the support of Mack's parents, I developed an individualized program for Mack to be implemented in his home with a team of instructors and therapists. We all met monthly over the span of many years, and I analyzed each developmental goal and added new goals to the program as Mack continued to achieve success. We worked alongside Mack's school once he entered kindergarten to ensure that each new environment of learning knew how to set Mack up for success.

"Fast-forward to today, and Mack is an amazing young adult who has achieved unbelievable amounts of success! His greatest achievement has been his willingness and commitment to being a learner. When he was a young child he worked tirelessly for hours each day on developing his skills, and as these skills improved we introduced different skills in areas such as communication, sports, and drama. As he became older, he began to take the reigns and initiate new goals based on personal interests.

"Being part of Mack's journey has been one of the greatest joys of my career. Mack is truly a remarkable example of how hard work and dedication can change the trajectory of a child's life. It is my hope that this journey will provide encouragement to families and children, as well as provide a framework for success in this growing developmental field."

Am Badwall
Mack's developmental consultant

"Although trying to improve our world can be overwhelming, keeping perspective and taking on manageable small things can be most impactful. We need to raise kids who know what their priorities are, and are confident enough to stand up for what they believe in."

Julie Cole, influencer
Co-founder of Mabel's Labels

Chapter 25:
I AM A NURTURER

Name:

Issabella, Mackenzie, Amelia, and Kaeden Patel

Ages: 11, 11, 9, and 7, respectively

Hometown: Currently reside in Vancouver, British Columbia

"Don't tell me the sky's the limit when there are footprints on the moon."

Paul Brandt

MY DREAM

Issabella and Mackenzie were born three months premature, so we have all been very aware about the importance of hospital care for children, particularly care for babies. That's why in 2016 we decided to raise money for the BC Children's Hospital. We spent the day making chocolate brownies and lemonade on Kitsilano Beach – and we sold out in 20 minutes! We couldn't believe it!

Since our food brought joy to so many that day, we began researching the correlation between nutrition and its impact on children's potential. We were stunned to learn some horrible facts about child hunger, such as how 100 million children in developing countries are underweight, 3.1 million children die each year from malnutrition, and 17 million children are born undernourished because of their mother's poor nutrition. We decided to do something to help change the lives of malnourished kids around the world, so we invested our monetary Christmas gift from our Nana and Granddad and created Give a Free Lunch, a campaign to ultimately serve one billion nutritious meals for kids who cannot get one.

MY SUPERPOWER IS COOKING

We realized that with small, fun activities and working together we could help others, even with just a lemonade stand! Since January 2017 we have planned an event each month in our community, such as selling lemonade in the warmer months and hot chocolate in the cooler months. All money raised is donated to organizations that are able to make a big impact, and so far we've raised enough money to feed almost 4,000 kids! We have raised $750 for Samridhdhi Trust, a non-profit organization that supports equal opportunity for education in India; $215 for a lunch program at a school in Vancouver by partnering with athletic wear store, ivivva, for a dance party; $350 with our lemonade stand in Kitsilano in August 2017; and over $1,500 from hot chocolate sales which we divided to Kids Against Hunger, KidSafe, and our local food bank.

Each of us has our own special ways of reaching our goals: Issabella manages our website, blog, and social media as our Chief Marketing Officer; Mackenzie sets the dates and times for meetings with companies, and holds everyone accountable for their commitments as our Chief Executive Officer; Amelia organizes our events and manages donated funds as our Chief Operating Officer; and Kaeden promotes our events as Director of Events.

We sometimes forget about our superpowers and roles – sometimes we just want to sit around and watch TV! Planning events is hard, and so is finding partners to help us, but together we have done a lot: we have strengthened our social media and technology skills, learned how to organize events, and we've improved our Math skills to total up our fundraising.

MY VOICE MATTERS

We donate all of our funds to organizations that help kids eat nutritious food. We always consider who we are working for, and hope that people enjoy our events, hot chocolate, and lemonade. We work hard but have fun, and most of all we are proud to help kids.

MY HEROES

Our support comes from our parents. Our dad helps us set our goals, talks about how we can work together, and teaches us that it's okay if we fail because we can learn even more from those experiences. Our mom supports us every day, making sure we eat healthy, arrive at school on time, and helps us get our supplies for each event.

My ADVICE TO YOUTH

Take a minute to think about how lucky you are, and then think about how you can help others.

To Adults

Support kids to be the best that they can be and to reach their potential.

"We knew that our children had a vision to make the world a better place during the Christmas season of 2016 when they said they didn't want any presents – they just wanted to share. Through their journey we've become more united as a family, and we are determined to leave a legacy that will motivate others to reach their potential and make the world a better place. We are proud that our children have learned so many valuable life lessons at their young ages: Issabella has learned how to cook healthy food; Mackenzie has learned to accept failure and move beyond it; Amelia has learned that hard work pays off; and Kaeden has learned how to listen and contribute. We don't have the perfect life, but we have had an extraordinary journey!"

Nina and Neil Patel
Parents of Issabella, Mackenzie, Amelia, and Kaeden

Chapter 26:
I AM A WATER ADVOCATE
Name: Autumn Peltier - **Age:** 13
Hometown: Manitoulin Island, Ontario

"What are you going to do about it?"
Auntie Josephine

MY DREAM

I live on the largest fresh water island in the world, and I am part of the Wiikwemkoong community, which values the sacredness of water. We value the water of the womb, and we acknowledge that we come from the wombs of all of our mothers. I know that nothing on Earth can live without water, and that our bodies are made up of 70% water. Our people honour and pray for water as it is considered a property of healing, and everything on Earth needs water.

Being First Nations makes me feel proud that I can represent and hopefully encourage more youth to stand up to save our planet. My vision is to help make the water of our planet so clean that we will be able to drink from the lakes and streams.

MY SUPERPOWER IS MY KNOWLEDGE

I became passionate about water advocacy when I was 8-years-old upon listening to my Auntie Josephine speak about the sacredness of water. She also spoke about all of the First Nations meetings, conferences, symposiums, workshops, ceremonies, and women's gatherings across North America where she shared her knowledge. Since listening to my aunt I have written speeches about water every year for the Native Language contest at my school, and I won three years in a row.

Writing about the importance of water for a school contest where your audience is predominantly children is one thing; writing about it for adults in important positions who can make impactful changes is quite another. I had to strengthen my knowledge with a lot of research, otherwise I knew I would not be taken seriously, especially because of my age. I spoke to the elders in my community, and I did my own research to learn about ways to protect water on a large scale. Through my research I learned about boil water advisories: public health warnings about contaminated drinking water. I discovered that some advisories were created close to Manitoulin Island because of an old uranium mine that leaked sediments into the water from Elliot Lake, causing people to become ill. I couldn't believe this! I was further dismayed to learn that over 25 First Nations communities in Ontario cannot drink their water, and over 200 communities across Canada – mostly First Nations – do not have access to clean drinking water. I didn't understand how this could happen in Canada, and I vowed to put a stop to it.

I spend a lot of time on my speeches, anywhere from a few hours to a few weeks, editing and perfecting it so that each speech is tailored specifically to the audience I'm addressing – and there have been quite a few different groups! I've done and continue to plan for many presentations for Chiefs across Canada; elementary, high school, and university classes; frontline workers such as healthcare workers and social workers; and First Nations ceremonies.

I posted all of my events and topics on social media, accompanied with photographs taken by my mom's friend, Linda Roy. Thanks to her and the support from local and provincial Chiefs, I began to garner quite a following, and soon provincial and national media learned of what I was doing. By 2015 I began to meet some very influential people, who further helped me spread my message, the first being Prime Minister Trudeau whom I met at a Chiefs meeting in Vancouver. Two years later I met environmentalist David Suzuki at a water symposium where we were both speaking, and I was invited by the youth Chief and Council from the Beausoleil First Nations to attend an environmental meeting at the House of Commons where I met Liberal MP Peter Schiefke.

I am imparting my knowledge with the world, and hopefully motivating others to change how they view water. It's not something we should take for granted. We need it to survive, and our planet needs it to thrive.

MY VOICE MATTERS

I've made some real positive changes in regards to water protection, but my journey has not always been easy. One of the biggest challenges I faced was being bullied by a group of classmates. They never talked to me, but they made fun of the work I was doing, and always within earshot. I could hear their teasing and insults, and sometimes those kids physically hurt me. I've also dealt with adults who tried to discourage me and even make fun of me, saying that I'm just a kid and kids don't belong in politics. It's sad that some adults think kids should not be heard. Adults should support and encourage us as we are the future leaders.

Sometimes I get a little overwhelmed by people who recognize me and swarm me. Other times I become stressed because my mom gets multiple requests from various places for me to speak, and I don't want to miss school. Sometimes I need to just be a kid. But after all that, I know that I am making a difference, and I am being acknowledged for it: I was nominated in April 2017 for the International Children's Peace Prize, and I have recently been re-nominated; I was awarded the Sovereign Medal in January 2018 at the Lieutenant Governor's Suite in Queen's Park in Toronto; and I received the Ontario Junior Citizens Award by the Ontario Newspaper Association in March 2018.

MY HEROES

I admire my Auntie Josephine, David Suzuki, and the Regional Chief for Manitoba, Chief Kevin Hart, for their advocacy work for the environment and their support to protect our lands. I am continuously inspired by David Suzuki's teachings, and I commend Chief Hart for his water advocacy for which he earned the Water Portfolio for the Assembly of First Nations, but Auntie Josephine is my biggest hero. She is my main teacher and inspiration, and I am honoured that I have learned and continue to learn so much from her.

I am also thankful for Wab Kinew, Chief Duke Peltier (my third cousin), Regional Chief Isadore Day, and – of course – my mother. Wab Kinew is the New Democratic Party leader of Manitoba, and he has encouraged me to enroll in law school when I am older so that I can eventually become a politician. Chiefs Peltier and Day, along with my community and Assembly of First Nations Chiefs, have supported me by helping me get my message out to influential leaders through allowing me to speak at Assembly meetings. Lastly, I am thankful for my mother because she organizes my schedule, drives me everywhere, and keeps me balanced by allowing me to still be a kid amongst all the water advocacy I take part in, such as letting me make slime, have sleepovers, and just have fun!

MY ADVICE

Water is sacred. Water is life. Mother Earth doesn't need us; we need her. We shouldn't have to fight for our water. We should just be able to have clean drinking water. Anyone can do the work I am doing and should be doing the work I am doing because we all need water to live.

"I am a single parent, and sometimes the financial challenge of travelling for Autumn's water advocacy in addition to everyday expenses can be overwhelming, but I am reassured of my choices when I see Autumn emulating the Anishinaabe-Kwe traditions and values I taught and modelled throughout her childhood.

"Autumn carries herself with a maturity beyond her years that is particularly admirable when she meets with our nation's leaders. Sometimes we suffer the emotional challenge of family separation: more often than not her sisters stay with family friends while Autumn and I travel, and Autumn and I must find the balance between work and family. However, when we return it is usually with gifts or part of an honorarium Autumn received, and we dedicate time to watching movies, baking cookies, car rides, and making slime, which benefits Autumn as well as she can relax from the seriousness of her endeavour.

"I will continue to support Autumn's cause, not just because she is my daughter, but because what she fights for is important for everyone and everything on the planet. Without clean water the planet will die. Every person of every race across the world needs to work together."

Stephanie Peltier
Autumn's mother

"Now more than ever, we need to inform young people about the issues happening in the world and share stories of resilient role models, people who are using their unique gifts, skills, and talents to make the world a better place. By believing in ourselves and learning what becomes possible when we refuse to let the bad news disempower us, then we, the younger generation can start trailblazing the path to a more sustainable and peaceful future. "

~ Kasha Sequoia Slavner, Award-winning Documentary Filmmaker, Social Entrepreneur & Founder The Global Sunrise Project

Chapter 27:
I AM AN ANIMAL PROTECTOR

Name: Jade Peter - **Age:** 10
Hometown: Napanee, Ontario

"Throw kindness around like confetti."
Anonymous

MY DREAM

When my family adopted my cat, Emma, from the Humane Society two years ago, I was shocked to learn that the staff relies heavily upon donations in order for the Humane Society to operate. I knew then that I wanted to help the Humane Society in some way, and I knew the perfect way how: through my different talents! I have loved to sing, dance, and model since I was little, and if I can turn one or more of my talents into a career when I grow up, then I will come back to Napanee and save all of the animals!

MY SUPERPOWER IS ENTERTAINING

I started dancing with Prestige Dance Academy when I was 2-years-old, and for the last two years I've been at the studio for an hour-and-a-half each week practicing hip-hop and lyrical. I have been enrolled with Mode Elle Model & Talent Agency since I was three, and since I was four I have been taking vocal lessons after becoming mesmerized by a singer at the Canadian Model and Talent Convention (CMTC). I have since performed at that very same modelling convention, created my own music videos of cover songs, sang the national anthem for our local hockey team, the Napanee Raiders, and sang "Jolly Old Saint Nicholas" for the *Hope of Christmas Volume II* album in 2017, which was produced through my singing coach at Elevation Music Studio in Kingston. I was able to sell those CDs for $20 each, and I profited $5 from every sale. I decided to use the money I made, which totalled $145, to help the Humane Society. I bought cat and dog treats, food and water bowls, different toys, and kitty litter – the Humane Society needs a lot of kitty litter!

MY VOICE MATTERS

Animals at the Humane Society need a lot of help, and so do the people who care for them. I've already raised over $100 to help them this Christmas, and next year I am hoping to give to other agencies, like the Sandy Pines Wildlife Centre and the Napanee Community Kitten Rescue. I've also started making catnip toys that I hope to sell at local markets and at veterinarian offices.

MY HEROES

My hero is Dr. K. from the show *Dr. K's Exotic Animal ER*. She's a veterinarian who saves the lives of pets by performing different operations. My favourite episode is the one in which she helped lemurs because the lemur is my favourite animal!

MY ADVICE TO YOUTH

You can make an impact just by doing small things, like giving money to a local charity, selling something you've made, or volunteering somewhere. Also know that sometimes life will be challenging, but if you keep going forward, you will succeed!

To Adults

You are the bigger people. You can do things with your friends or colleagues to make a big impact on the world. Also, remember that kids are inspired by whoever is in their lives. Be a positive role model, and help kids with their dreams.

"Jade has always had a very soft spot for animals, but especially in the last couple of years since the adoption of our cat, Emma. I am blown away by her maturity at her young age to help the furry friends in our community through her talents. After profiting the way Jade did from her CD, I'm sure a lot of kids would have bought toys or candies, but not Jade. It was such a powerful moment when she dropped her purchases off at the Humane Society. At just 10-years-old, she has learned amazing life lessons, such as caring, sharing, honesty, and love, and once we have those values we don't get rid of them. They are character traits for life.

"She was also able to achieve one of her dreams already: to be recorded on a CD and being able to profit from her talents. I believe this is something she will do time and time again. She shows kids that they can do whatever they put their minds to."

Becky Lloyd-Peter
Jade's mother

Chapter 28:
I AM A HAPPY SOUL

Name: Pip - **Age:** 5

Hometown: Canada

"'Ohana' means 'family.' 'Family' means 'no one gets left behind'."
Lilo (*Lilo and Stitch*)

MY DREAM

My dream is for everyone in the world to feel included, loved, and happy.

MY SUPERPOWER IS BEING MY BEST SELF

I have Down's Syndrome, but I don't let that stop me from doing what I want! I play with my brothers and my puppy; I love dancing and listening to music; and I can do lots of things that my doctors once told me that I couldn't do, like reading and talking.

MY VOICE MATTERS

I teach people every day how to have a happy soul and to love. My mom even created an organization called the Happy Soul Project where I tell my story. I now have lots of people around the world – including the U.S. Marines – supporting me, wearing my Happy Soul Project shirts, and ordering my calendars, which features kids with differences.

MY HEROES

My family is the most important thing to me. I also love my grandparents, classmates, educational assistants, and teachers. I hold them all near my heart.

MY ADVICE

Be happy to be who you are. Everyone has something great about themselves that needs to be shared.

"A few weeks after Pip was born, as I put her in her crib, I looked up at a sign that I had made for her that read: 'Life is more beautiful because you are here.' After putting Pip to bed, I fell to my knees and wept, grieving for the life I thought my daughter was going to have.

"I had to learn many skills, such as putting tiny contacts into her eyes, caring for her after her different surgeries, and managing her type 1 diabetes and celiac disease. However, through her I also achieved my vision of espousing the values that are truly important to me: equality, inclusion, acceptance, and love. Because of my little girl, I created the Happy Soul Project, an organization devoted to celebrating differences and inclusion.

"The Happy Soul Project is an entrepreneurial non-profit organization that operates a shop run by students with extraordinary needs. We also have various projects and programs such as our worldwide #differentisbeautiful campaign that has brought awareness to hundreds of vast and rare disorders; our calendar that features over 60 kids who have overcome many obstacles, including Pip; 'Be Awesome Today', which inspires thousands of people around the world each month to go out and do something awesome for someone else; and our 'Kick-It-Capes' Project that has given over 6,000 personalized superhero capes to kids facing a terminal illness.

"Pip is here for such a powerful purpose, and through the Happy Soul Project I hope to change other people's perspectives so that everyone can celebrate their differences."

Tara McCallan
Pip's mother

"Our youth heroes are here and ready to inherit this divine planet of beauty, and we (as mentors) can be part of the change that is on the horizon by consciously nurturing our youth with peace, love, music, and leadership."

Greggory Hammond, influencer
Author, Teacher, Musician,
Founder of The Global Jam 4 Peace
Director of Make Music Day (Washington, D.C.)

Chapter 29:
I AM RESILIENT
Name: Avery Plumb - **Age:** 15
Hometown: Delhi, Ontario

"Mount Everest isn't something you conquer. It's something you dance with."
Sebastian Sasseville

MY DREAM

Like many teens who begin high school, I was intimidated. The school was big, there were many new faces, the workload was harder, and there was the constant scramble of getting from one class to another on time with the right books. A month after I started, something else happened that added to my anxieties: in October 2017 I was diagnosed with type 1 diabetes, meaning that insulin, the hormone that controls sugar in the body, is not produced, and my sugar levels can spike or drop dramatically. To prevent this from happening I learned to monitor my sugar levels by pricking my finger and testing my blood with a medical device called a glucose metre. I also have to eat or drink something every time my sugar levels are too low, and take insulin injections four times a day every day.

I became the diabetic kid in my high school. My peers looked at me funny, or made jokes whenever I checked my blood sugar or injected insulin. I grew tired of having to explain the disease over and over again to make my peers understand what I was going through. I wanted to hide the fact that I had this disease so I could avoid the teasing and repeated explanations, and I became resentful. Why were kids with glasses or hearing aids exempt from teasing, but I wasn't? I needed my glucose metre and injections to help me function, just like kids who can't see well need glasses, or kids who can't hear properly need hearing aids. I knew that if I kept quiet about my disease I wouldn't help myself or any other kid with type 1 diabetes, so I decided to bring awareness about type 1 diabetes so that children can be more accepting of this disease.

MY SUPERPOWER IS SPEAKING OUT

The hardest thing to remember is that people who are ignorant about type 1 diabetes are not ignorant by choice. They're not surrounded by it, so they don't know about it. I knew that I could make a difference in the mindsets of my high school peers if I could raise awareness. I started researching about cures and preventative measures about the disease, and I have learned to be more vocal whenever someone teases me or gives me strange looks. Now, instead of laughing at me, my peers ask me questions, and I am treated much better!

MY VOICE MATTERS

Bringing awareness about type 1 diabetes has already eliminated any misunderstandings my peers had about the disease, and I know that if I continue on my path I will allow for more support for those with type 1 diabetes. I have made an impact in my high school, as well as in my elementary school where I returned to deliver a presentation so students would not grow up ignorant about the disease. I also mentor a 13-year-old girl recently diagnosed with type 1 diabetes whom I met through a friend. We often chat about diabetes, and I answer any questions she has. In June I will take part in the Brantford Walk for a Cure, and I look forward to volunteering in the future with my diabetic team at the Brantford General Hospital.

I am so happy and amazed with how I've managed and adjusted to this diagnosis, and I can't wait to bring that feeling to others with type 1 diabetes!

MY HEROES

My mother is my hero because she is a strong person who raised my sister and I all by herself. She keeps me focused and makes sure I'm on track in managing my diabetes. I also admire my grandmother because she is there for my family. She calls my sister and I every day after school to check up on us and see that we're okay.

My friends from high school have been very supportive on my journey, and they even participate in finger testing to check their sugar levels to make me feel more comfortable.

Lastly, Mrs. Stacy Green is my hero. She was a teacher at my elementary school, and while I never had the pleasure of being her student, I spent a lot of time with her because of our involvement with a social and emotional wellness program introduced in our school called the Compassionate Crew Program. She was the lead coordinator, and I often helped her with assemblies. As I got to know her, I discovered how compassionate and resilient she was, and she gave me great advice when I expressed anxieties about starting high school. I now look to her as a dear friend, not just a teacher.

MY ADVICE TO YOUTH

Stay positive, always look forward to the good things in life, and never change who you are. If you are not familiar with diabetes, please educate yourself to be more accepting and understanding.

To Adults

Always be there for kids through the good and the bad, and allow them to have a voice and to express their feelings.

"Avery and I became acquainted through the Compassionate Crew Program. She spent several recesses with me supporting the program, either by making posters for special events, or practicing for skits for the assemblies she was part of. Even though I never had the opportunity to teach her, we became teammates, not only because of our work with the Compassionate Crew Program, but because we are both diabetic. I am type 2 diabetic, and Avery has given me the courage to talk openly about my disease by sharing the struggles and hopes that she has.

"I told Avery when I first met her that she should forget about the people who cause her stress and anxiety, and to focus on herself. Since then she has developed her own approach towards challenging situations, and has taken the initiative to develop her voice amongst youth, something I am especially proud of as she used to be very shy.

"Avery is a prime example of how communication – the good, the bad, and the ugly of all conversations – is key to lasting change. Communication saves lives. There is help everywhere, and if you just find one person to reach out to, you will be well on your way to getting the help you need because you are not alone. Put away your devices. Talk at the dinner table. Do not use social media to compare yourself to others. Keep your eyes in your own heart with your loved ones."

Stacy Green
Avery's former social and emotional wellness coach

Chapter 30:
I AM BRAVE

Name: Meriel Reed - **Age:** 16
Hometown: London, Ontario

"One person can make a difference. Together we can change the world."
Saidat

MY DREAM

I have a severe medical phobia that I believe is the result of my medically complicated birth. I was delivered by an emergency C-section because my heart rate dropped too low, and within minutes of being born my lungs were suctioned, I had IVs inserted for antibiotics, and I was given oxygen, all due to meconium aspiration syndrome (MAS), an inhalation of meconium and amniotic fluid. My mom was told that I had a 50% chance of making it through the first night, and for the first four days of my life I was away from my mom in a specialized nursery.

When I was 10-years-old, I developed a kidney condition and later a thyroid condition, both of which require regular monitoring. Any test or examination gave me extreme panic attacks: I would scream all the way to the clinic and fight like a tiger to get away from any doctor who tried to go near me! Just the mention of anything medical would trigger a panic attack. My phobia damaged my self-esteem because I was embarrassed of not being able to control my behaviour. Thankfully, over the last few years I have worked closely with a Child Life Specialist, Erika Clements, as part of the Child Life program at Children's Hospital in London to help me manage my phobia and I am making progress.

Through my time at Children's Hospital I have seen many children face chemotherapy, and I can completely relate to their feelings of fear and discomfort because of my medical phobia. I wanted to help them, but I never knew how until I met Nicole Snobelen, founder of The Abby Fund, a charity that creates princess dresses and superhero capes that sick kids design. In 2015 she sewed me a beautiful gown, like something out of a dream, which made me feel like a princess for the Magical Winter Ball, an event held at the hospital for which I was the guest speaker and singer. As I got to know Nicole and learned more about The Abby Fund, I became truly inspired by the quiet way she went about brightening the lives of sick children. I knew that I wanted to make a difference too, just like Nicole. I now work as a Patient Ambassador for Children's Hospital, and I speak at fundraising events. However, more than that, I have become impressed by the bravery of sick girls I have seen in the hospital. I want to help them find a way to feel positive about what is happening to them, or at least distract them from their suffering, if only for a short while.

MY SUPERPOWER IS SEWING

While speaking as a Patient Ambassador for Children's Hospital in October 2015, a video was shown of a sick girl who was getting chemotherapy treatment. She smiled beautifully through her pain, and I instantly admired her bravery. Shortly after the event, I drew a sketch of a head covering I wanted to make for her. I showed it to Nicole, and she suggested that I consider designing and sewing head coverings for girls with cancer.

Her idea was amazing, but the project proved to be a very big one. It was a challenge to maintain my focus while doing my schoolwork, and there were so many things to learn. I had to research cancer treatments that caused hair loss, the impact hair loss had on people, and which types of fabric to use specifically for skin affected by chemotherapy. I had to learn a lot of sewing skills too, like following a pattern, adapting patterns, and working with linings, and I had to learn how to create a website and promotional materials like videos. It took me a full year to do my research, write my proposal, and organize all of my materials, and it took many trial sewing efforts before I achieved any kind of success. My first efforts were pretty awful! I had to try to stay focused on the girls I wanted to help, and I touched base with Nicole whenever I was really struggling.

My success far outweighs the challenges I faced. First, my superpower has allowed me to make progress on managing my medical phobia. Second, my superpower has had a huge impact on my life as I started my own charitable project called Gypsie for which I design and sew head coverings for girls with hair loss due to cancer treatment. So far I have donated 37 head coverings, and some have even gone as far as Guyana! Finally, my superpower has helped me become perseverant and empathetic: I had to be very persistent to get my charitable project going because I had to learn many new things and it was quite a process, and my empathy was strengthened as I was so motivated by my project.

I feel really happy whenever I see a photo of someone wearing a head covering I sewed, and I was incredibly proud to speak about how my charitable project was inspired by and has grown from my experiences with Nicole and The Abby Fund at a fashion show fundraiser for The Abby Fund in June 2017.

MY VOICE MATTERS

The best advice I have received came from my school song: "The secret of living is loving and giving. Everyone needs roots and wings." We sang these words every week during assemblies for eight years, and they are truly words that guide my life. I love and give to the girls I make head coverings for, and I know that my small act is making a world of difference to them. Cancer tried to take their beauty when it stole their hair, but I gave it back to them and boosted their confidence!

MY HEROES

Some people think of heroes as superheroes, but I think that ordinary people can be the most extraordinary heroes. Nicole Snobelen is both my fairy godmother and mentor who inspired me and helped me start my charitable project. She gave me so much good advice on all aspects of the project, donated big bags of fabric and ornaments, and always encouraged me so that I continued to try even when things weren't going so well. Most of all, I have been so encouraged to watch Nicole face and gradually overcome a fear of her own: public speaking. If she can conquer that fear, then there is hope for my medical phobia!

Erika Clements, my Child Life specialist, is an extremely compassionate and patient person who has worked hard to help me manage my medical phobia. She is an angel to sick children in the hospital, and her kindness inspires me to try the impossible. She also has her own fear of public speaking, and she tells me that I am helping her manage her fear.

My other heroes include my grade school teacher for many years, Erin Poirier, who guided my growth and development into the person I am today; the brave girl from the hospital video; and my voice instructor, Lesley Andrew, who has had huge success in her career despite being faced with the challenge of having a learning disability. Singing is one of my passions, but Lesley doesn't just teach me how to sing: she inspires me to dig deep and make the most of life, and she's a motivational speaker on behalf of those with learning disabilities.

I am also extremely thankful for my friend, Mckenna Lumley, who is also featured in this book and has faced some really serious medical issues. I met Mckenna at the Magical Winter Ball the year I spoke, and there was an instant connection between the two of us. We have been good friends ever since, and she has even modelled some of my head coverings for her promotional materials for her book, *The Secret Portal*, about the power of imagination.

These people all care about those around them, and they don't just *feel* compassion but they *act* to show that they care. The roots of my life have drawn nourishment from the lives of my heroes. Their influence has given me the wings I need to soar through life by loving and giving, the only way to live a truly happy and fulfilling life.

MY ADVICE TO YOUTH

Every single one of you has something you can do, big or small, to help someone else. Many little things add up to big change in the world. Don't assume you can't just because you're young. Take time to look around you, and you will find someone who needs you.

To Adults

Let children find their passion and then help them achieve it. Believe in them – they can do it!

"I met Meriel through my charitable project, The Abby Fund, which is dedicated to lifting the spirits of children suffering from illness. I volunteer my time to meet with them in the hospital to design their dream dress or superhero cape, which I then bring to life and gift to them. I had the pleasure of taking Meriel's dream dress design and bring it to life for the Children's Health Foundation's Magical Winter Ball in 2015.

"I knew there was something special about Meriel when I first met her. Learning that she wanted to use her talents to better the lives of others is so inspiring because she uses her experiences to help others, whether that is sharing her story or using her gift of sewing to brighten people's lives. The work she does means something, and she is not only a role model for many young girls in our community, but she has already impacted my life in many ways. Her kind and generous heart is a constant motivation to be the best version of myself that I can be, not only for myself, but for the people who may look up to me. I spend a lot of time with children who are going through the most difficult times in their lives, and it's important to me to be a positive influence and to inspire these kids.

"I want to encourage people to follow their dreams, believe in themselves and inspire others. I believe Meriel is a wonderful example of this!"

Nicole Snobelen
Meriel's mentor

"No matter how far gone we may feel at times, there's always a way to turn your pain of the past into the beauty of the future."

Matte Black, influencer
Founder of Heroes in Black

Chapter 31:
I AM MOTIVATED

Name: Lauren Reycraft - **Age:** 17
Hometown: Cambridge, Ontario

"A river cuts through rock, not because of its power, but because of its persistence."
James N. Watkins

MY DREAM

Like a lot of teens out there, my first job was at McDonald's. It was great and flexible, allowing me to concentrate on my studies, play competitive volleyball for Guelph, and hang out with my dog, Lola. But I eventually started thinking, "What about after? What am I going to do for the rest of my life?" Then, in grade 11, I got my golden ticket to my ideal future.

I took a marketing class, and for our culminating project we had to create our own festival. I came up with a three-day music festival called F.L.O.: Future Like Ours, which incorporated a variety of different musicians to express all the diverse personalities of young adults. I received 92% on this assignment, and realized that a career in marketing was my dream. It still is: I hope to be a well-known woman in the marketing world and share my ideas about the difference it makes when you are motivated to do the things you love.

MY SUPERPOWER IS DIGITAL MARKETING

My high school volleyball coach, Owen Jones, once told me: "You can do anything you want because in the end the only person stopping you is you." There are a lot of people out there that are on the fence about whether or not they should strive for something much bigger than they think they are capable of. I strive to be a leader to those people because I believe that you can do anything with 100% effort and commitment. I can deliver this message to thousands of people at once – even millions – if I am successful at digital marketing. I could impact the world because the more motivated people are to reach success, the more people will do to create a better world. While I am still learning organizational skills needed for events and projects, I have already organized events for my volleyball team that have brought my team closer together, like going out for dinner, or going to watch university volleyball games. I have helped one group of people collaborate – I am excited to see what I can do on a global scale!

MY VOICE MATTERS

I am really proud of the fact that I never really got into drama in high school. Instead of using my voice to spread gossip that everyone dreads in their teenage years, I pursued my dream. There is so much negativity in the world, and time is too valuable to waste on that. I would rather be a team leader to steer people in the right direction. The world would be a better place if everyone understood the language we commonly know as love.

MY HEROES

My hero is my mother, who passed away from cancer when I was 12. She pushed me into playing all kinds of sports, eventually driving me to play the sport I am best at: volleyball.

A while after her passing, another wonderful woman came into my life, Marisol, who married my dad. She too has pushed me to do so many good things for myself, including the opportunity of sharing my vision in this book.

A huge shout-out goes to my dad, Keith, for always having my back and raising me to be the person I am today. I would never be as good at volleyball as I am today without him driving me to and from practice every day.

MY ADVICE

To Youth

If you are ever feeling like something you are doing isn't worth it, take a step back to remember what your goal was in the first place and strive for it. We all have highs and lows, but just remember where your spark of inspiration came from. Nothing is set in stone until you are, so lead the best life you can lead for yourself and others. The difference is all up to you. *You* create your own reality, *you* decide what's best for *you*, and *you* are the person who knows *you* best.

To Adults

Every adult has their "do's" and "don'ts", but those shouldn't get in the way of kids' "wants" and "don't wants". Let kids explore what they feel comfortable with, and that will guide them towards their future hobbies and jobs. Let youth be youth while they are young.

"Because of the death of her mother when she was a young child, Lauren sometimes felt that life wasn't really worth living. I had to help her through those thoughts and to help her understand that it doesn't matter how much time you have, but what you do with the time that is given to you. I have a feeling this helped her become motivated to find her purpose.

"I never thought I would be a mother, so raising Lauren has been a major blessing. I realize that love is strong and deep, and that you don't need to be of the same blood to be completely in love. I love Lauren with all my heart. I saw her light up in her marketing class. She built brands and products, and shared her projects with such enthusiasm and passion that I knew she found her purpose – and she has been accepted into the marketing program at Fanshawe College!

"Our world can be anything that we want it to be. It has the potential to evolve with just a thought or an intention. I know that Lauren's attitude and aptitude can and will change the world as she is a leader and will lead humbly and kindly. She will create the future that the world is so desperately in need of, one that is positive, kind, loving, and accepting. I wish that more children can discover their purpose, and I hope to help people own their throne in life. You are everything that you need to be. It's all inside of you. Don't listen to anyone but yourself and your heart, and bring that to the world. We are all kids at heart. We still have our same dreams we had when we were younger. Honour them. Listen to them. In those dreams is your true purpose, and when you learn to listen and honour them, you will bring out the real you."

Dr. Marisol Teijeiro, ND
Lauren's stepmother

Chapter 32:
I AM GIVING

Name: Adonie and Lydia Sacallis
Age: 13 and 10, respectively
Hometown: Red Deer, Alberta

"Not doing it is certainly the best way to not getting it."
Wayne Gretzky

MY DREAM

Adonie

When I was 4-years-old I was at a big outdoor festival where there was a giant piñata full of candy for over 100 children. When we broke it open we all scrambled to collect the candy as it fell to the ground. I got three pieces of candy, but the boy beside me didn't get any, and he started crying. I gave him two of my pieces and he became happy. His parents were very surprised I gave away more than I kept for myself. My mom was super proud of me and grateful that I was so kind to the younger boy. I learned then how great the feeling of giving is, and I wanted to give things to people who didn't have what I had. My dream is to motivate people to do the same.

Lydia

Before the end of school in 2016 our mom asked us what we wanted to do during our summer vacation. I thought back to the summer before when we had gone to Europe, and then I became sad because I realized how lucky I was to travel when so many kids aren't able to. I then started thinking of all the other kids who don't have necessities, like food and clothing. Even now I sometimes become sad going through grocery stores, thinking about people who are not able to afford food. Every day I am reminded of how privileged I am. I want to see a world where everyone can have anything they dream of, and I believe we can have such a world if we all just learned to share.

MY SUPERPOWER IS GIVING

In the summer of 2016 we started a charity called Just Give. Our goal was to visit 12 countries in 12 months and raise money for various charities in each of these countries. Our mom took us out of school for a year and she helped us teach others how great it is to just give!

In October of 2016 we helped a nonprofit organization called Dove Mission in the very poorest part of the Dominican Republic by giving people food, materials for crafts, and school supplies like printers. It was so great to make friends and see them smile.

The next month we travelled to Mexico where we helped a community centre for orphaned children by purchasing a working toilet and painting murals all around the centre to brighten the atmosphere. Most importantly we spent time with the kids. We taught them English and showed them how to make crafts. After Mexico we went to Costa Rica, France, Spain, Italy, and Greece, as well as Vancouver, Halifax, Charlotte-town, and Toronto, to share our ideas of giving. We learned that giving feels good and that everyone can give from their hearts.

One of the scariest moments we had travelling was in the Dominican. We were giving out Boxes of Joy, care packages filled with food, school supplies, toiletries, and a few small toys for kids who don't get to go to school. There was a massive rainstorm, and many people told us to get off the streets, but we were determined to help these kids. It was so scary and cold, and the streets were running with water, but being wet was way less important than those kids who had nothing to eat, so we trudged through the storm and delivered all the boxes! It was worth it to see their faces when we came through their doors.

MY VOICE MATTERS

We take so many things for granted here in Canada, something as simple as toilets and food. It's strange and sad to think that so many people in the world don't have basic rights. We met a lot of kids who have had nothing to smile about, and when we shared with them they had blank looks on their faces. Their caregivers told us that they forgot how to smile, and so we did all we could to remind them. To make them smile again was worth everything. Giving feels amazing, and it feels better than getting!

We're proud that we can bring real change to people around the world, and we have talked about our experiences in different schools across Canada and the places we travelled to. We want kids to know that giving from the heart costs nothing, and most of the time it means everything. We still continue to give, though now in our community through the donation of clothing and recycling bottles.

MY HEROES

Our parents are our heroes. They divorced when we were young, but they have grown to still be great friends. They're so intelligent and hard-working, and they never give up when life gets tough.

We are especially thankful for our mom. We were homeschooled for a year as we travelled to different countries to raise money for charities and share the important message of giving. Our mom always teaches us more than what we need to know to get good grades. She teaches us life lessons.

Adonie

I admire hockey player Alex Ovechkin because he does good things for people, like skating with young kids, and one time he gave his stick to a fan for his birthday. He is strong and determined, and he has been awarded with so many trophies for his efforts, some of which he won more than once, like the Rocket Richard Trophy, which he won six times for having the most goals in a season, and the Ted Lindsay Award, which he won three times because of his outstanding performance to the judges of the NHL.

Pinball Clemons is also my hero. He was a very famous football player in the CFL, and we were inspired by a campaign of his charity foundation, Just Give. When we found out about it, we reached out to him and even met him in Toronto! We tossed a football around and went to his big Charity Gala where we were invited to help give awards on stage! He didn't have to do any of that because he didn't know us, but he just gave to us from his heart.

Lydia

I look up to YouTube actress Liza Koshy because she isn't afraid to be herself. Even when someone gives her a negative comment, she turns it around to find humour in it. She knows how to make people laugh, and laughing is the best way to connect.

MY ADVICE TO YOUTH

Be yourself and the right people will be drawn to you. We are all special and we all deserve to be ourselves. Sometimes on the road to happiness we might make some mistakes, but accept failure as a teacher, not as a punishment.

To Adults

Teach kids to give to others, even if it's just a high-five or a pat on the back for motivation. Remember: we are just kids and we don't know what you know, so use a kind and loving voice to help us get to where we need to be.

Giving

"I was incredibly moved when Adonie and Lydia approached me with the desire to raise money for various charities over their 2016 summer break. Lydia also added the condition that we had to personally deliver money and items to the charities so we could ensure these things were going directly to the people in need. She then went on to ask, 'Why don't more people just give?' It was such a fantastic question, and that much more profound coming from a child. She and Adonie raised the inarguable truth that we all have the capacity to give, and some of the best things we can give to enrich the lives of others don't even cost money, like a hug or a smile or a simple greeting to a stranger on the street.

"Helping them live out their vision is now an everyday thing we do as a family. Their idea to just give is such a simple one, and I have learned so much from them. In 2016, I sold my house and car, moved most of my possessions into storage, and travelled with my children for a year to help those less fortunate than ourselves. We faced floods, hurricanes, windstorms, lost luggage, and struggled with language barriers. I faced criticism from family and friends who thought my actions stupid. Some of these people even took to social media with their judgments, but my children's courage and kindness completely overshadowed these challenges.

"I am so proud that both of my children are so focused on making the world a better place at such a young age. We felt like superheroes, flying around the world to help people in need, and my wish for the world is for everyone to don their superhero capes and go out and make a difference!"

JB Owens
Adonie and Lydia's mother

"With persistence, our greatest challenges in life can and will become our greatest successes."
Eli Brown, influencer, CEO and Founder of Shine the Light On

Chapter 33:

I AM PEACEFUL

Name: Griffin Searle - **Age:** 9
Hometown: Stone Mills, Ontario

"Kindness begins with me."
Clara W. McMaster

MY DREAM

My dream is to turn bullies into good people because there are too many bullies in the world who ruin our chances of peace. It isn't hard to be nice to others, or to want to help people who need it most.

MY SUPERPOWER IS MY SIGHT

When I was 3-years-old, one of my eyes started looking towards my nose, and my vision in that eye just got worse. I was told I had strabismic amblyopia. I got glasses, as well as an eye patch over my good eye so that the vision in my bad eye was forced to get stronger. When I started kindergarten that year, I looked different from my peers, and because I looked different I was sometimes teased. I didn't like to wear my eye patch very much, and I was happy when I didn't have to anymore. I was bullied all over again when I switched schools after my family and I moved. One boy was especially mean. He threw ice at me, and one time he blocked the way up a snow hill that my friend and I were trying to climb.

To him and bullies like him, I was the kid who couldn't see. They were wrong. I *can* see, just not in the way they think. I can see these bullies for who they really are: kids who are sad, angry, or scared inside, or kids who have hurt feelings. Because I can see people for who they are on the inside, I have the courage to speak out against bullies, like the time the bully at my school blocked the snow hill. I stood up for my friend and I, and the bully let us pass! Now he doesn't bother me!

MY VOICE MATTERS

It's so much easier to be kind than to be mean. I have never looked at anyone different from me with a negative attitude the way the bully at my school looked at me. I use my superpower to see who these people are, and I find a way to help them.

One group I always help is the homeless. Last year for my birthday, I didn't want any presents, and instead my mom and I collected donations to give to a local mission. We raised enough money to feed 100 people!

Why can't bullies think like that? Can you imagine how the world could be if they replaced their mean actions with nice ones? Bullies have made me feel motionless and afraid, just like how I am sure the homeless feel. If bullies can change their mindsets, then they can help bring peace to the world.

MY HERO

My heroes are my hamsters, Sky and Snowflake; my dog, Cally; and my fish, Snivey. My hamsters have both passed away, but they taught me how to be gentle because they were so small. I was always careful with them, and now I'm that way with other animals, including Cally. Snivey is so relaxed. He swims slowly and takes in the scenery. He taught me to be calm and enjoy the simple things in life.

My friends and family are also my heroes because they have accepted me for who I am.

MY ADVICE TO YOUTH

Don't hurt others.

To Adults

Don't be too bossy. Make sure everyone around you has a good life.

"When we make the decision to become a parent, we make a conscious decision to become fully responsible for another human being. We never know in that moment what that means exactly, but parental instincts kick in, and we all of a sudden live with our hearts outside of our bodies. We become protectors, advocates, and biggest fans.

"My heart ached for Griffin after he was diagnosed with strabismic amblyopia. Upon entering kindergarten, he was upset on many occasions because other kids had been mean to him. I was sad to discover that bullying was happening regularly in his school – and it seemed to be an issue faced by parents in general.

"A few years later we moved and he began a new school. The teachers and staff are amazing, and Griffin fared better because his cousin and neighbourhood friends attended the school as well, so he had a good support system.

"Bullying isn't new. I'm sure every adult can remember a time, or many, when they were younger and were victimized. What we should focus on are the positive attributes of children, and really encourage them to step into their own true potential. If kids can learn to love themselves and accept their differences at an early age, then we will all be better for it.

"Griffin's dream is to make everyone feel loved and accepted. I think that is why he became concerned for the homeless. I remember one afternoon when my boys and I had stopped off at a gas station: we saw a homeless man, and Griffin and his brother decided to give him their two bananas that they had packed as a snack. From then on, Griffin questioned why there are people in the world who have nothing, while we have so much.

"My husband and I are extremely proud of Griffin. His heart is in the right place to want to help humanity. We love him and his brother dearly."

Jen Fitzpatrick
Griffin's mother

Chapter 34:
I AM A SINGER

Names: Celia, Annie, and Aryana Siriopoulos
Ages: 14, 12, and 10, respectively
Hometown: Markham, Ontario

"Be yourself; everyone else is already taken."
Oscar Wilde

MY DREAM

Just like the Sister Sledge song: we are family! Not only are we sisters, we are a singing trio! Our band name is Caardia, which is inspired by the first initials of our names and a tribute to our Greek heritage as the word "cardia" in Greek means "heart". We have always loved to sing pop songs, but when we found out from our vocal coaches that we actually had good singing voices, we knew that we could turn our hobby into a dream come true!

Our dream is to one day become singers who will help people globally overcome their challenges through our music.

MY SUPERPOWER IS SINGING

There are so many musicians in the world today that promote inappropriate messages in their songs, and these songs are unfortunately listened to and taken seriously by young audiences. These musicians have so much power to create change and they're creating the worst possible kind! Well, God gave us good singing voices, and we are determined to use them for the greater good!

Our music has already strengthened our bond as sisters. We learned to listen to each other, and take everyone's opinions and perspectives into account before making any big decisions. We want to take these lessons to the world: we pay attention to what's going on in the world every day, which continually motivates us to keep writing and singing about anything and everything that matters.

We've already had many performances, such as the Taste of Danforth, the Toronto Christmas Market, Pride TO, Pure Philanthropy Gala, and the Salute to the Olympians such as Andre de Grasse. We are also Celebration of the Arts bursary winners, and we have appeared on CP24 Breakfast Weekend, Rogers TV, and Global News.

Like every superhero though, we've had our letdowns and our troubles. People who we thought were our friends have bullied us and refused to support us. When we released our first video for "Love, Hate Thing", our classmates put our video on our class SMARTBoard and openly made fun of it. We decided to switch schools, and we wanted to keep our singing career private in case we were criticized again. As time went on though, we learned about an anti-bullying organization called Kill it with Kindness, and we have been speaking in front of schools about our experiences and to help others shine – what a turnaround!

We refuse to back down because some people don't like what we do – we want to help people, and that's what counts.

MY VOICE MATTERS

We only write songs that have important meanings about issues prominent in the world today: "No Breakdowns" is about bullying; "Way Home" is about finding out who you are and being true to yourself; "Soap" is about deciphering lies from reality; "Deep End" is about how we lose our way because of our dependency on cell phones; and "Overs" is about getting over loss.

So many people have told us after our concerts or on our social media pages that they have gone through similar challenges as illustrated in our songs, and we will continue to let people know they are not alone, as well as continue singing and speaking about popular world issues.

MY HEROES

Our parents are our heroes. Both keep us constantly happy and are very selfless, making so many sacrifices for us by putting us before themselves. They provide us with the opportunities we need to achieve our goals in life, and they are very motivational and want us to do well in whatever we pour our hearts into. They're the foundation of us and we build from their morals and values in life.

Canadian Idol judge, Zach Werner, was our first vocal coach and is one of our heroes, too. A family friend referred us to him in 2014, and he started us off in our career: he gave us impromptu concerts in different parts of Toronto, and he took us busking out in the streets to get comfortable with performing in front of people.

After Zach moved to Newfoundland in 2016, he referred us to his friend, Michelle Newman, who became both our vocal coach and our angel. She has complete faith in us and wants us to succeed more than anything. She believes in our individuality and our personal journey. She loves the fact that we're sending out our own positive messages, and she always reminds us to never forget who we are.

Finally, Jesus is our hero because He died for us and helps us every day.

MY ADVICE TO YOUTH

If you don't love what you're doing, it's not worth it. You only have one life, so do what you love.

To Adults

Listen to what kids have to say and learn from them.

"I am blessed to be the mother of these wonderful girls. They are spreading some extremely positive messages like anti-bullying, self-belief, and female empowerment. I want my daughters to grow up to be empowered, strong, positive, and able to make their own decisions to lead a very fulfilled life, and if they can help others, even better. It's my job as a parent to help them succeed as best they can. All adults should be supportive to children because they are the future, and children need to follow their dreams, educate themselves, and align themselves with people who will make their dreams come true."

Lisa Siriopoulos
Mother to Celia, Annie, and Aryana

"These young souls are the game-changers, the way-showers, the warriors of light who will change the world for the better. They have the energy and the imagination to create what we need to thrive again as a global community. They know that they cannot wait for someone else to sort things out. I would encourage every young person to tell their story, whether it be through words or images or music. If by telling your story, you help someone else make sense of their life, or feel encouraged to express their own story, then you have made a difference."

Michelle Gordon, influencer
Author of Visionary Collection

Chapter 35:
I AM A LEADER

Name: Marlow Slatter - **Age:** 12
Hometown: Belleville, Ontario

"A true hero is not measured by the size of his strength, but by the strength of his heart.*"*
Zeus (*Hercules*)

MY DREAM

In 2017 my teacher, Mrs. Mulhall, selected me to attend the Students as Researchers Conference at the Ontario Education Leadership Centre (OLEC) due to my leadership role in the school community. OLEC is an outdoor camp located outside of Orillia that is centred around engaging and educating youth to maximize their potential as leaders by encouraging them to positively contribute in their schools, community, and beyond. Our cumulative task was to bring a research question to our school and make a change in our school based on the results. My team of four students chose "How do extracurricular activities affect student happiness and motivation", and after surveying the students in our school and implementing the extracurricular activities they suggested, we discovered that our strategies worked to create a happier school community. Students were more engaged because they were given the opportunity to create and lead extracurricular activities that they were passionate about, and stress was taken off staff members who tried to run so many different clubs.

I want to continue to use my voice for change, ultimately helping kids realize that they all matter and have voices that deserve to be heard.

MY SUPERPOWER IS LISTENING

One skill I really needed to work on in the beginning of my journey was listening. I became so focused on being a great leader that I would often disregard those around me, thinking that I knew best, and I took over different initiatives. I needed to learn to really listen to those around me, not just hear what they said, but also understand them. After all, how was I supposed to speak for people if I didn't listen to them? Some leader I would turn out to be!

I strengthened my listening skills through my research project, and what was once a weakness is now my superpower. I am completely committed to making my school a better place for both students and teachers. I have listened to those around me and I ensure their voices are heard. For example, through my research project I asked students what extracurricular activities they wanted. Our school already had a few, but I wanted to make sure a variety of different opinions and interests were represented. The project began offering clubs for Lego, robotics, games, sports, art, and drama.

Through listening to those around me I am able to respect diverse opinions, and convey these opinions with conviction and passion. Now people are listening to *me*, and noticing that I can make a difference.

MY VOICE MATTERS

My research project impacted my school community in a very powerful way. My research team submitted a proposal to SpeakUP, a project devised by the Ministry of Education's Student Voice, which aims to promote student engagement and success in Ontario schools by listening to and learning from students. If we are chosen, we can be awarded with a grant of up to $2,500 to help our project make more of a difference in our school.

I have also applied for the Ministry Student Advisory Council, which is a group of approximately 60 students from all parts of the publicly funded education system across the province. If I am selected, I will be able to share my ideas with other students on the Council and provide advice to the Minister of Education.

I am really proud of myself for taking on a big a project that made such a huge difference in so many lives in our school community. It not only positively impacted students, but their families and our teachers and staff as well. Our school is a happier place because everyone's voice has been heard.

MY HEROES

My heroes are my parents, brother, and my cousin, Nick Foley. My family members are my biggest supporters, and they always make sure I have everything I need to be successful.

Nick has inspired me to be a leader through his example. When I was 3-years-old, he gave me a rock with the word "COURAGE" on it. He told me that when I was scared I was to hold this rock, and courage would be with me always. Whenever I'm scared or in need of bravery, I always hold the rock close, like the time a former figure skating coach told me I was not good enough. I kept that rock close to me every day and slowly healed from that challenge and learned to believe in myself again. I'm not the only one who uses the courage rock either: my mom holds it during my figure skating competitions!

Lastly, Mrs. Mulhall is also my hero. She is a passionate leader in our school who spends countless hours providing opportunities and suggestions to make my project better, and she challenges me to push my boundaries. I was so proud when she approached me and expressed her surprise and appreciation of the success of the project.

MY ADVICE TO YOUTH

You can achieve anything you set your mind to. If someone tells you that you can't do something, don't be afraid to say: "I can do it – just watch me!"

To Adults

You are setting an example for children. We learn from our leaders, especially parents and teachers. Never tell a child that he or she cannot do something. We are capable of so much – we will surprise you!

"I remember an early morning when I was dropping my child off at daycare, and as I was driving I saw Marlow and her dad running together. That really stuck with me because the hour was so early, and yet there Marlow was, starting her day with fresh air and exercise to better her personal excellence. She is a prime example that age doesn't matter when it comes to making change. When young people do inspiring things, other young people are influenced to do inspiring things too, and the world becomes a better place. I want to see Marlow succeed, and my hope is to offer her any kind of guidance that I can by sharing my experiences and life lessons. I hope more young people can be like Marlow, and embrace every day as a new opportunity to positively influence our world by understanding who they are and allowing their best selves to come out in how they live."

Nick Foley
Marlow's cousin

"During her nine years as a student at Our Lady of Fatima School, Marlow has contributed to both the school and wider community as a disciple of Christ. She consistently and selflessly gives herself to others, and her words and actions serve as a role model to her peers. She is an active member of the school community, and she fulfills many volunteer roles such as a choir singer, peer monitor, and eco-club member on a daily basis. All of these roles require a great deal of maturity and responsibility, and I know for a fact that several of our primary students rely on her guidance. Each day she models the theme 'Be the Change' by being friendly, considerate, respectful, and helpful. When students need help socially or academically she is quick to offer advice or help in a supportive manner. Many teachers have had their day brightened through a friendly conversation out on yard duty, or through the exchange of kind words in the hallway. Teachers can trust her, and they know she will demonstrate maturity and positivity toward whatever task she is given. I cannot be more proud to be her teacher!"

Mrs. Mulhall
Marlow's teacher

Chapter 36:
I AM UNSTOPPABLE

Name: Abby Springham - **Age:** 14
Hometown: Delhi, Ontario

"You miss 100% of the shots you don't take."
Wayne Gretzky

MY DREAM

There are so many people around the world, including here in Canada, who struggle to get basic rights that are so easily taken for granted in most First World countries, things like food, clean water, plumbing, and shelter. I am one of the lucky ones: I have all of these things, as well as a family who loves me, friends who support me, and a right to education, which many girls in Third World countries die trying to achieve. I have the opportunity to play sports and travel; to eventually drive as I get older; and to work in any career I choose. I know how fortunate I am. I know that I have a life full of opportunities that many are not able to have. Because of this realization, my dream is to travel the world to help people in other countries who are less fortunate than me.

MY SUPERPOWER IS KINDNESS

Right now I am making small differences when I can, but those small differences have huge rewards for the people I am helping. For example, during a trip to Ottawa in January of this year, I saw a woman experiencing homelessness sitting on a street, and as it was a very cold night, I gave her my gloves and a bit of money. She was so appreciative! Whenever I go to London where my brother, Willy, has regular appointments at Children's Hospital (he had cancer six years ago), my family and I buy food from grocery stores that we give to the homeless. Even though my acts of kindness are small, they still help people in great need. If I can do a lot of small acts all around the world, I am sure I can help make the world a better place.

MY VOICE MATTERS

Before I can reach my dream, I have to overcome my shyness – how am I supposed to help people if I get a bit nervous talking to them? I try my best to overcome this, usually by grabbing any opportunity to speak in front of crowds. I've done this twice at my elementary school with my brother. We had a social and emotional wellness program there called the Compassionate Crew, and every year beginning in January our school held a five-month charity initiative called Dragons' Dreamworks where we picked any charity we wanted and promoted it in the school. Willy and I took part in this twice: once for the Therapeutic Clown Program at Children's Hospital, and once for Toronto SickKids. We chose those charities because both hospitals helped my brother and our family when he was sick, and Willy really connected with a Therapeutic Clown named Ollie who we still see whenever Willy has a check-up. Near the end of both school years, we presented our charities and explained to a panel of judges why they should win part of the funds raised. Willy and I were lucky enough to win a few hundred dollars for each charity!

MY HEROES

My family, friends, and volleyball teammates are all important to me. My family and friends are always there for me, and my teammates push me to try to improve so that I can be the best that I can be.

I admire my grandparents for having the ability to make people laugh and smile, even in tough situations. They do things out of the goodness of their hearts without ever expecting anything in return, and they are always there for my family without complaint.

My other hero is Stan Goch, who runs Simcoe Xtreme Volleyball Club where he volunteers his time to help kids play volleyball and stay active. I used to play for Simcoe Xtreme, but I wanted to try out for the Woodstock Warriors Volleyball Club as it was more competitive. Stan encouraged me to do so and I was lucky enough to make it! Stan continues to watch me, and he offers constructive feedback so I can improve my game.

My family, friends, and Stan Goch always talk to me like I'm capable of doing great things in life. I'm so lucky to be surrounded by positive people!

MY ADVICE TO YOUTH

Work hard in order to achieve your goals. You cannot wait for things to happen. You have to do things yourself to get things rolling.

To Adults

Allow children to do what they want to do. You can be there to help and support them along the way, but you have to allow children to follow their dreams.

"I recognized Abby's selflessness the first time I met her. Her sincere kindness shows in her everyday acts. I have witnessed Abby encourage others by letting them go first in volleyball drills and by being a positive role model. She shows humility, handles criticism well, and is always looking to improve herself. To see the core value of putting others before oneself in Abby makes me want to assist her in any way possible to achieve her dream to help the less fortunate. Abby – just like every other child out there – has the potential to do whatever she wants to in her life by staying focused and never giving up. We all make mistakes; that is how we learn. Abby is well aware that hard work is needed to achieve goals, and I believe she will greatly contribute to making the world a better place by being a positive influence on her peers."

Stan Goch
Abby's former volleyball coach

"Young people in our community have shown me time and again how skilled, passionate, and driven they are about the issues we face, and about how they want to be leaders in delivering solutions. I was just a kid when I first toured Parliament Hill and thought, wow, I want to work here someday! Dreams do come true with hope and hard work, and low and behold, here I am after many years of building experience and connecting with and working for my community. My message to young leaders today is: aim high and work hard. We believe in you, and you too can fulfill your dreams."

Mike Bossio, Member of Parliament for Hastings—Lennox and Addington

Chapter 37:

I AM FORGIVING

Name: Ryedr Squires - **Age:** 10

Hometown: Waterford, Ontario

"I am here to serve. I am here to inspire. I am here to love. I am here to live my truth."

Deepak Chopra

MY DREAM

I hope that street drugs will disappear off the face of the earth because drugs destroyed my family. My dad is an addict, and because of his addiction my siblings and I don't see him every day like other kids see their dads regularly. I still love him though, and I hope I can teach kids the dangers of drugs so they will never turn to them in the first place. I also want to teach addicts the impact their choices have on others.

MY SUPERPOWER IS STORYTELLING

In grade three I was given the chance to educate others about drug addiction. My teacher gave us an assignment to create our very own superheroes, and I decided to tell my story and raise awareness about drugs in this assignment through a character I called Captain Maple, who turns street drugs into maple trees. I also used some teachings I learned in religion period. Religion is my favourite subject because it makes me feel calm and I have learned forgiveness. I used to be angry and hurt with my dad, but I still loved him, and through that love I learned to forgive him.

My teacher allowed me to present my story to my class, and I was allowed to talk about my dad being an addict. Presenting was great because I communicated my message to kids my own age so that they could understand what I was going through. Most importantly, I taught that while there are a lot of reasons why someone might turn to drugs, their bad choices don't make them bad people.

What started out as a class assignment has helped me deal with the loss of the family I once had with my dad, and I hope to one day get my story published to help other families who have been broken by drugs.

MY VOICE MATTERS

Drug use is a global problem. Sending someone to jail for selling drugs is not a solution to get people to stop using drugs. The only way to stop drug use and drug dealers is to teach kids when they are young about the dangers of drugs. We all know that drugs can hurt you, and even kill you, but what kids don't realize is that drugs break families and break the spirit of those affected by a drug user's choices.

I started teaching about the dangers of drugs and the effects of drug addiction on families and kids when I was in grade three, and I hope that through my story I can prevent kids from turning to drugs as they get older.

MY HEROES

My mom is my hero because she is always there for me. She also helped me create Captain Maple. She respects me, and she is loyal and kind-hearted. She has a beautiful personality, and she makes me feel loved.

MY ADVICE

Don't take drugs. If drugs don't kill you, they will ruin you, your family, and your friends.

"One of the biggest challenges I faced was accepting that my husband and the father of my children was an addict. I became a single parent because of his decisions, but supporting Ryedr with his vision helped me come to terms with the changes in our lives.

"Educating and helping others is sort of a family trait: Ryedr comes from a long line of psychiatric and addiction nurses. I am a registered nurse in mental health and addictions, so my son's vision is also my vision personally and professionally. Ryedr's dream came from a difficult time in our family, and I am proud that he is using a painful experience to make positive changes for others. Helping Ryedr achieve his dream will help bring more detox and rehab facilities to communities, and prevent people from starting to use drugs in the first place, thus making the world a happier, healthier place.

"I hope that more affordable treatment centres for people battling addictions will be made available. Currently we do not have the resources to help people battle addiction. Sometimes people go to detox centres for a short period of time, and then have to wait months to get into a treatment program after. This is not ideal because they then have to wait on a list for months to learn the skills needed to maintain their sobriety.

"I am proud that Ryedr has compassion and wants to make changes so that others don't have to experience the same pain he has endured."

Rayvin Squires
Ryedr's mother

Chapter 38:
I AM A MASTER TEACHER
Name: Mia Tansley - **Age:** 6
Hometown: Paris, Ontario

"You get what you get and you don't get upset."
Victoria Kann

MY DREAM
My dream is to help other people have a good life. I'm so happy, and I want other people to feel the same way I do. I want to share what I know about being a Master Teacher and teach it to the whole wide world!

MY SUPERPOWER IS TEACHING
My Gym teacher, Ms. Vallieres, taught my class about how to be healthy in our bodies, minds, and souls. We were her Master Students, and she was our Master Teacher, but she also introduced us to lots of other Master Teachers in pictures, stories, and by bringing in cute stuffed animals. My favourites were Oliver, Coach Wolfie, Marvellous Monster, and Twilight. Oliver was a fluffy cat that taught us to use our imaginations; Coach Wolfie

and Marvellous Monster taught us about how being nice is better than being mean; and Twilight taught us how to be peaceful.

I like being a Master Student because I get to sit and listen, but I like being a Master Teacher more because I get to help my friends. To me, teaching is showing people things instead of telling people things, and when I'm being good my friends follow me and they are good too.

MY VOICE MATTERS

I loved learning about the Master Teachers so much that sometimes Ms. Vallieres let me take over her lessons! I taught in my kindergarten class, and now I teach kids in my grade one class about all the things I learned from the Master Teachers, like sharing, meditation, exercise, and friendship. I'm becoming a Master Teacher so fast because I teach my family and my class with my beautiful words.

MY HEROES

My parents are my heroes because they help me follow my heart, and Ms. Vallieres is my hero because she taught me all about the Master Teachers, and now I get to be just like her.

I also look up to Oliver, Coach Wolfie, and Marvellous Monster, but Twilight is my most favourite Master Teacher. She is a unicorn that taught me how to sparkle! She doesn't hold onto any anger and instead lets all the bad stuff go so she can let her love and peace shine. That's the kind of Master Teacher I want to be.

MY ADVICE

My advice to everyone is to spread love and peace everywhere so people can feel it and give it, too!

"I was in my third year of university when I had Mia. I was 21-years-old. Some people might think that becoming a young mother would instigate years of regret; that I may have missed out on many opportunities and put important goals like education on the backburner. This simply was not true. Though it sounds cliché, having Mia helped me grow into the person I am today. Motherhood brought out the best in me in all aspects of my life. I became a better student and achieved grades in post-secondary education I never thought I could. I finally understood that my capabilities didn't depend on what others said I could do, but what I believed I could do myself.

"Raising a girl in this day and age can be tough: girls are surrounded by provocative media and so many fallacies about beauty. I will have to explain that equality wasn't always the norm, and ensure that Mia doesn't become aware of some harsh realities too early. It is important for me to build Mia's self-esteem, and to raise a confident girl who will blossom into a confident woman, proud of who she is. I want her to spread her positive message to other youth as doing so will start her on a journey with endless possibilities. Having the opportunity to be grouped with such an esteemed group of heroes is a wonderful start to Mia's education!"

Emma Tansley
Mia's mother

Chapter 39:
I AM CONFIDENT
Name: Rosemary Tarzia - **Age:** 13
Hometown: Thunder Bay, Ontario

"Live, Love, Laugh, Dream."
Anonymous

MY DREAM

I was bullied when I was in grade three. I knew that it wasn't normal to make people feel like less of a person because of what they looked like, and I knew that everybody is equal and deserves to be treated with respect.

As a result of that experience and how hurtful it was, I want to make a positive impact on other kids who may be going through similar experiences. My dream is to help kids affected by bullying understand that things get better with time, hard work, and patience.

MY SUPERPOWER IS MY COURAGE

In grade four I was asked by my teacher to create a video showcasing my experience of being bullied for an education conference. I spoke about how I felt when I was targeted with mean-spirited words and behaviour, and I identified strategies that children and teachers can employ when dealing with students who demonstrate aggressive behaviour at school. Two years later I received the Principal Award for my leadership skills, and I currently sit on the Student Council where I help organize different fundraisers, assemblies, and school events for important causes like bullying.

I am stronger than I thought I was, and I've learned that when you set your mind to something, even if the results don't always turn out as planned, there will always be other opportunities.

MY VOICE MATTERS

I have learned to be fearless and to speak the truth. I stand up for what is right, and I give people the courage to keep going when they feel like they can't go on. This makes the world a better place because people will start to believe in themselves and be more confident, which will allow them to do whatever they want and achieve their dreams.

MY HEROES

My parents and grandparents are the most important people in my life because I know that no matter what they will always love and support me. They give me strength to continue to help others.

My other hero is Ellen DeGeneres because she loves and accepts people just as they are. She tells people to be kind to one another, which is exactly what I believe. I think the world would be a better place if we were accepting of all people and treated all people with dignity and respect.

MY ADVICE TO YOUTH

Never let anybody – whether it be the unkind kids in your class, teachers, or even your parents – tell you that you're not strong enough, confident enough, or unable to achieve your dream. If you believe in yourself and in your dream, then what you want will come true. Never forget to believe in yourself.

To Adults

Support is the number one thing children need. Watch what kids are doing and not just saying because you can learn things from both their words and behaviours. You won't know this if you aren't paying attention.

"Rosemary has emerged as a leader within her school community, acting as a compassionate authority on bullying prevention and serving as an agent for positive change. I've always encouraged Rosemary to follow her heart and the little voice within her. I've taught Rosemary that her inner voice acts as an inner compass that will point her to the pathway of her best self, thus placing her on a trajectory for success.

"I believe in the importance of working in service of others, especially those who are vulnerable, and I think that belief system set a strong foundation for Rosemary. I am the Program Supervisor for our North Region with the Ministry of Children and Youth Services/Ministry of Community and Social Services. My work aspires to create a fulfilling future for the citizens of Ontario, and Rosemary is working towards the same goal, which makes me so proud.

"I have also done research to support Rosemary, such as a six-month online course about the science of wellbeing. I taught Rosemary about the psychology of success and the pathways of human flourishing to support the evolution of her growth as a whole person body, mind, and spirit. Lastly, when I acquired a Masters Degree in Leadership Studies, I taught Rosemary about leadership behaviours she could employ in her own life on a daily basis.

"As Peggy O'Mara stated: 'The way we talk to our children becomes their inner voice.' Rosemary has taught me about being attentive, and she reminds me to act out of love, not fear, and to listen to my heart. She has taught me about having the courage of my convictions, and to speak my truth assertively and with compassion. Rosemary is a natural leader, someone who challenges the status quo in an effort to make the world a better place."

Marnie Tarzia, MA
Rosemary's mother

"She raises every day with an energy that radiates a sense of purpose that tells her that It is the truth; she has purpose and It will find her, just don't give up on It. Don't lose hope. She will figure It out. It has been assigned to her before her first breath. One day, she meets It. An illumination takes place that brightens her community and impacts the world. She realise that her obedience to persevere in her actions was calling her purpose to herself all along. She is loved. She is relevant. She is value without measure. In her and through her others find worth. She is hope."

Opa Day, influencer
Founder/CEO of Empowering the Teen Spirit Wellness Center

Chapter 40:
I AM A DREAMER

Name: Hannah Thompson - **Age:** 12
Hometown: Hamilton, Ontario

"We are all made of all those who have built and broken us."
Atticus Poetry

MY DREAM

I have loved to sing and act since I was four and sang at a family Christmas party, and my dream is to sing and act on stage and in films.

MY SUPERPOWER IS MUSICAL ACTING

I've had a blast playing Zuzu in *It's a Wonderful Life* and Gretel in *The Sound of Music*, both at Theatre Aquarius. I also played Fiona in *Shrek: The Musical* as part of the Hamilton-Wentworth District School Board's co-op program, ArtSmart, in partnership with Theatre Ancaster. I got to use my superpower while also gaining high school credits! Finally, I played Annie in the musical of the same name at Theatre Ancaster. *Annie* particularly has changed my life because I was taught some great singing techniques from my vocal coach, Erin Bree Pierce.

I hope to one day bring my talents to the world and bring happiness to people the way performers like *Stranger Things* actress, Millie Bobby Brown, bring happiness to me. Entertainment brings so much joy to people, and it makes them forget about their problems. Musical acting has helped me overcome challenges. My parents divorced when I was ten; I was often picked last in sports or activities, or left out altogether by my peers; I moved six times and went to five different schools; and I have had audition rejections. Without my superpower, I don't know how I could've gotten over all that, but I did! I want to bring that kind of strength to others.

MY VOICE MATTERS

I am really proud of my evolution as a performer. I have a stronger singing voice, more confidence on stage, and because of both of those qualities I am now a better performer. I've learned that failure is a part of life, and that I should always put a positive spin on things that don't go the way I planned. For example, if I don't get a part that I auditioned for, I think that the part wasn't meant for me and I simply move on because there's always more roles I can try for.

MY HEROES

Millie Bobby Brown is my hero because she is an amazing role model and actress at only 14-years-old. She is pursuing a wonderful career, and is basically living my dream.

Erin Bree Pierce is also my hero because she has done a lot with her life. She's a performer, director, and vocal coach in musical theatre, and she coached me throughout the whole production of *Annie*. Erin helped me through a lot during the play, like teaching me vocal warm-ups and techniques to strengthen my performance and helping me manage my stage fright. I'm so thankful to have her in my life.

MY ADVICE TO YOUTH

Be your yourself and don't listen to any negativity.
To Adults
Let kids have a voice!

"I was thrilled to meet Hannah during the production of *Annie*. I knew we were going to get along great, and that we could learn from each other and put our best foot forward in the roles we were playing together. Hannah's personality shone right through from the moment she was cast, and when she came to my studio for private coaching I was able to see more of that spunky personality. I was amazed at how she handled herself in this production. Her talent alone was one thing, but to be able to pace herself and take direction the way she did, and to work with adults and children, was truly remarkable. It is rare to find a child of that age who understands the responsibility of leading an entire production. The weight of that is huge! She took the entire production on her shoulders and rocked it every single show and rehearsal. She worked so incredibly hard, and that's a quality that is to be admired and cherished. I have great respect for the level of maturity that Hannah displays.

"Hannah will impact the world. She is infectious, focused, and positive about everything life has to offer her. She's very driven and welcomes any challenge that is thrown her way. These are the qualities that will take her places in many years to come. She is inspiring, not only to her own age group, but adults as well.

"She is the real deal. What you see is what you get, and what you get is pure joy and awesomeness! I will forever remember *Annie* as the time I met Hannah, the kid who played Annie; the kid who rocked every single show; the kid who made me laugh; and the kid who gave me hugs backstage. Hannah is exquisite and a real treasure for anyone who has the opportunity to work with her or, in some way, be in her life."

Erin Bree Pierce
Hannah's vocal coach

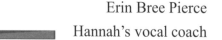

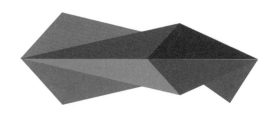

Chapter 41:
I AM AWESOME

Name: Jeron Van Dyk - **Age:** 11
Hometown: Tavistock, Ontario

*"Share the magic in your heart. There's nothing you can't do. Oh, anything
is possible, so find a dream inside of you."*
Mickey Mouse

MY DREAM

I gave my mom a good laugh when she asked me what my dream was. I told her my
dream was to create a Value Village. Other people may have thought I meant the store,
but my mom knew what I meant. I meant a *village* that *values* all differences, whether
they are physical or mental. I want the world to be like Heaven because sometimes, well,
it hasn't been that way for me.

I have autism, and I have trouble communicating. I know what I want to say in
my head, but when I try to say the words, it doesn't work. I've memorized a lot of movie
scripts and song lyrics to help me say what's on my mind. Sometimes people get im-

patient with me, and then I get impatient with them because they don't understand me. Things can get really frustrating really quickly, but when I have people like my family who understand, my life becomes easier. That's why my dream is to create a "Value Village" of differences, which my family and I have done at Spectrum Acres. It's a place near Stratford, Ontario that my family and I created with the intention of peace, love, acceptance, understanding, happiness, and fun.

When we can understand one another, we can live peacefully.

MY SUPERPOWER IS TRANSFORMING NEGATIVITY INTO POSITIVITY

It's a bird! It's a plane! It's SUPER JERON, with the power to make people happy and be easy to get along with! I can connect and change people for the positive, and when someone is having a bad day, I can feel that bad energy and help transform it with my positive attitude. An example of this was at my Opa's funeral: there were lots of people there and everyone was spread out, so I kept walking around the crowd in circles, making everyone move closer together and closer to my Opa in his resting place. By doing this everyone drew on each other for comfort.

When I help others transform their emotions, it may look like I am in another world or doing a crazy dance. I feel everyone's emotions and mirror them. This makes people aware of how they are coming across. Simply by being aware of what emotion someone else feels allows that person to question why they are feeling that way and how they can manage it. Once people can understand their own emotions, they can better understand the emotions and needs of others like me.

MY VOICE MATTERS

While I have trouble putting my thoughts into words, I have a super amazing device that helps me: my Spell-2-Communicate board! I have been able to share *my* ideas using *my* words, even if the words don't come directly from my mouth. For example, I had an idea to have a statue of my school saint, St. Ambrose, built in the playground as a reminder for all who see it that St. Ambrose is the patron saint of school children. I may not have been able to say what I wanted to say, but thanks to my board, I could communicate with my principal, and now the plan is getting in the works! Even while I might not be using my actual voice, my voice still matters.

MY HEROES

St. Ambrose is my hero because he had a powerful way of speaking, and he was said to be "honey-tongued". St. Ambrose shows me that even though everyone has a different way of communicating, everyone has a message and everyone's message needs to be heard.

MY ADVICE TO YOUTH

We all need to claim our place in the world. Everyone has a story, and you need to be brave enough to share yours. Also, come visit Spectrum Acres if you can! We have had some great events for people like me and their families to feel totally at home.

To Adults

Enhance the lives of kids so they have something to contribute, and make sure to listen to them. One day I was told to get off the computer and I said, "I'm sorry. I've got important things to do. This is important to me." My parents understood, knowing that even though what I was doing didn't look important to them, it was to me and they trusted me.

"When Jeron was first diagnosed with autism, I was grieved, but through the grace of God I was able to see my son for who he truly is. Everyone has a special place on Earth, and everyone, no matter the label, has something to contribute to make Heaven on Earth.

"The most important, powerful thing for me is to help Jeron become accepted for being, not disabled, but differently-abled. He hammered this point for me when he was just 6-years-old. He played the song 'Lead Me' by Sanctus Real repeatedly until I understood his message:

'To lead them with strong hands
To stand up when they can't
Don't want to leave them hungry for love
Chasing things that I could give up
I'll show them I'm willing to fight
And give them the best of my life
So we can call this our home
Lead me, 'cause I can't do this alone.'

"Then he topped it off with a verse from 'Home' by Phillip Phillips: 'Just know you're not alone/'Cause I'm going to make this place your home'. This led to the creation of Spectrum Acres, a place where Jeron and others like him can feel at home by interacting with each other while simultaneously connecting with nature on the farm.

"To help me connect with my son and those at Spectrum Acres, I took courses in Awesomism, a program developed to understand autism, and I am now a Level III practitioner. I am also a Kids Coaching Connection coach, meaning I am trained to help children become more prepared for life.

"I am a firm believer to love everyone on your path, especially those who are different. They are the ones we grow from. At Spectrum Acres we are impacting kids and adults with special abilities by helping them realize that they are unique and offer the world something very special. The world needs their gifts and abilities in order to evolve. Jeron described it as 'Apocalypse', which means 'change' in Hebrew. They are here to help change the world quickly.

"My constant prayer is to assist God in creating Heaven on Earth, and I know that God is using my son to reach this goal."

Anna Van Dyk
Jeron's mother

"Youth look at the world and are more and more disconnected from their grander community as technology plays a deeper role in shaping their realities. But nothing can beat in-person connection, true connection, which is what the youth of today crave more than anything else."

Miguel Lopes, influencer
Founder of BeBrightEyes

Chapter 42:
I AM OPTIMISTIC

Name: Barath Velmurugan - **Age:** 15
Hometown: Brampton, Ontario

"Be passionate and bold. Always keep learning. You stop doing useful things if you don't learn."
Satya Nadella

MY DREAM

I have been interested in the business world since I was 14-years-old. I was fascinated by economics, and I knew I wanted to play a key part in boosting our country's goods, services, and jobs. I had not the faintest idea of how to do this, so I began reading biographies about successful people in business to draw knowledge from their experiences. I became motivated by the inspirational stories of these people, and I started comparing myself to them. They were driven and determined from a young age, whereas I, like many youths today, spent too much time distracted by my cell phone. Not only did this dilute my focus and any goal I tried to set, it also affected my health. I spent more time communicating with people through my phone than I did in person. My happiness depended on any notification I received, and my phone became like an extra appendage. I began noticing how those around me were almost robotic, transfixed on their phones and oblivious to everyone and everything around them, and I learned how cell phone radiation was cancerous and even affected the environment.

I realized that I didn't want my head down at a screen, but up in the world – the business world to be precise. I wanted to leave a mark like the people I read about, so I decided to improve myself. I enrolled in career development courses, and I volunteered at CARABRAM, a multicultural festival in Brampton. I also volunteered at a March Break camp hosted by PointClickCare, a cloud-based software company that supports senior care providers. My dream is to become the CEO of an organization that focuses on the betterment of the environment, specifically in regards to global warming and climate change created by human activity.

MY SUPERPOWER IS PRESENTING

Presenting is not just standing in front of a crowd and stating a bunch of information and statistics. Each presentation requires organization skills to compartmentalize ideas; time management skills to limit stress and ensure practice of my presentation; and communication skills so that my audience understands my message. I also want my audience to be engaged for a length of time, so I often use PowerPoint slideshows and accompanying videos that I find online, and I culminate with a discussion period to ensure understanding and reflection.

I understand that I have to be unique from competitors to be more successful, and the first step in doing this is to thoroughly understand the topic I am presenting about. Whenever a project or challenge is given to me, I first explore the details and make emotional connections to gain empathy from my audience about my message. I use recent data to make my presentation as relevant as possible, and I include quotations from prominent figures in the world. Most importantly, I tailor my presentation to whomever I am speaking to. I know that if my words are too complex for a young audience, or too childish for an older audience, then my presentation will be dull, and it will be even more painful to listen to if it is dragged out for a long period of time.

I always bring energy and enthusiasm into whatever presentation I do, and I try to tell a few jokes when I can. I am always improving my ability to create a good relationship with my audience.

MY VOICE MATTERS

I have done many school presentations for various subjects, and I have also volunteered my time to speak at different events. At CARABRAM, for example, I led presentations on cultural instruments and antiques, and I have been nominated as the Star Speaker for Brampton's Youth Leadership Program Milestone's event due to my bi-weekly presentations for the Program about environmental issues such as plastic misuse, global warming, and endangered species. I also received first prize for the Plasticurious Video Contest in 2017 (ages 14 to 15 across Canada), conducted by the Canadian Plastics Industry Association. This contest fused my love of presenting and my passion for the environment, and it challenged me to reflect on my use of plastic items in daily life.

I am proud of my accomplishments and experiences thus far, and I look forward to what awaits me in the future.

MY HEROES

CEO of Microsoft, Satya Nadella, is my hero because he never allowed any negative thoughts to overtake him during his career. His consistency in performance and skills in innovation, management, and communication guide me with a clear view on what I should do in life to succeed.

MY ADVICE TO YOUTH

Hard work is always important, no matter how smart or talented you may be. Everyone has something to contribute, so never forget what makes you unique, and use your uniqueness as part of a team.

To Adults

Never tell a child what to do, but offer advice and support, especially when they begin to plan their careers.

"When his beloved son was convicted of a drug charge in 2015, kung fu actor, Jackie Chan, never used his celebrity status to influence the release of his son, but rather expressed that his son should realize that everyone is equal under the law.

"I admire Jackie Chan for being a morally responsible father. There are so many parents who refuse to acknowledge the wrongdoings of their children, and instead blame others for their children's actions. Such perspectives allow their children to become lazy, self-entitled, and irresponsible, values that I refuse to instill in my children.

"Barath has been a hard-worker since he was a young boy, and I am proud that his goal to become a successful business leader is motivated, not by money or power, but by the impact he could have on society and the environment. His aim is to solve the pain of the people, and I am proud that he has discovered his inner hero so early in life.

"I am a firm believer that hard work never fails. Any mistake one makes is a learning experience, and any success is a triumph."

Velmurugan Thavasi
Barath's father

"Music is one of the few activities we do as humans that utilizes both sides of the brain: the logical left side and the creative right. When children learn to play music at an early age, the extra neural connections generated help them to be more success-ful, both in school and later in life, no matter what career path they choose. Music is also something we can feel deep within our bodies and soul whenever we listen to our favorite songs. These feelings can help inspire youth to pursue their own dream of dreams, essentially awakening the inner hero inside them."

Vincent James and Joann Pierdomenico, influencers
Authors of "88+ Ways Music Can Change Your Life"
Founders of Keep Music Alive, Teach Music Week (3rd week in March),
and Kids Music Day (1st Friday in October)

Chapter 43:
I AM DETERMINED
Name: Kaelin Woods - **Age:** 9
Hometown: Paris, Ontario

"We do not need magic to change the world, we carry all the power we need inside ourselves already. We have the power to imagine better. "
J. K. Rowling

MY DREAM

I like to dance, figure skate, swim, write, act, play ukulele, and hang out with my friends. At times though, these things can be very hard to do because I have anxiety. Most people see a friendly, confident girl, but there are many times I am super nervous, even when there's nothing to be nervous about. I panic. I pace. I cry. I feel like I'm going to lose control, and I just want to be at home. It's a terrible feeling.

My dream is for people to be more understanding when someone is feeling anxious, and I hope to share my story with my school community, the town I live in, and eventually kids around the world. I want others with anxiety to feel comfortable coming out of the shadows to speak to people without being afraid.

MY SUPERPOWER IS MY DETERMINATION

My first panic attack happened during the summer before I entered grade one. I was at my grandparents' house with my family, and I was running around outside when my parents told me to slow down. I immediately started freaking out and I just wanted to go home. I don't know the reason for my panic attack – I was with familiar people in a familiar place – but for a long time after I didn't like being anywhere away from home.

Until this past year I had fairly regular panic attacks. I called home from school at least once a week, and a lot of times I even went home. I didn't want to join any teams, or go to any parties or sleepovers. Whenever I had an anxiety attack, I felt embarrassed and I didn't want people to see me like that. I still feel like that sometimes, but I am slowly overcoming my anxiety. I recognized that my common triggers are when I join a big group at a social event, or if I am asked to do something I have never done before. I have developed some coping strategies to help me whenever I am in one of those situations: I give my coaches a heads-up whenever I join a sports team; I distract myself with reading and writing stories; I become more involved at my school in order to force myself out of my comfort zone; and I ground myself during any anxiety attacks by quickly thinking of five things I see, hear, and feel. Anxiety tries to stop me from doing the things I love, but I am determined not to let it win!

MY VOICE MATTERS

I want to help those with anxiety realize that they are not alone in their struggles, and one way I hope to achieve this in the future is by taking part in Heads Together, a mental health campaign created by The Duke and Duchess of Cambridge and Prince Harry.

I became interested in the Royal Family when I was 3½-years-old after watching part of the Queen's Diamond Jubilee on CBC with my mom. My mom explained the celebration to me and I understood it to be similar to a birthday party, so I wanted to send the Queen a card. My mom wrote out what I wanted to say and I included a picture of myself. I was so shocked when we got a reply just a few months later! Then I sent Prince Philip a card after I heard that he wasn't feeling well – and I got another reply!

What started out as an interest became therapeutic for me after my anxiety began. Writing to the Royal Family and waiting for their replies gave me something exciting to think about and look forward to. I write to them for birthdays, anniversaries, holidays, new babies, weddings, and sometimes for no specific reason. Then I learned about Heads Together, which lets people know that it's okay to get anxious. I admire the work the Royal Family does through that campaign, and I hope to share with them my idea of kids helping kids with anxiety through my letter writing.

MY HEROES

My heroes are my Uncle Adam (who passed away), my teacher, Ms. Tancredi, my parents, and my brother, Keenan. My Uncle Adam taught me to never stop fighting, no matter what life hands you, and I admire Ms. Tancredi because she taught me to never stop doing the things I love. My parents and Keenan teach me how to lead a happy life and stay focused to achieve my dreams.

MY ADVICE

If someone is experiencing anxiety don't just say, "It's going to be okay." That doesn't help, and it makes the person feel like his or her anxiety is not a big deal. Anxiety *is* a big deal to people who experience it, so please listen to what they are saying, reassure them by valuing their words, and talk to them about what they're thinking and feeling

"I have witnessed Kaelin develop from a quiet and shy student into a talented and confident musician. I used to tell her to play louder because her timid notes were a reflection of how she felt about trying something new in front of a person she barely knew. Now, Kaelin performs full songs for me, singing and playing at the same time. With each verse and chorus, I gain even more respect and appreciation for her determination.

"Over the past 13 years, I have taught students all over New Brunswick, Alberta, and now Ontario. Connecting with heroes like Kaelin is a rare occurrence as she shows the dedication needed to be successful and to accomplish the goals. I always say that I have the best job in the entire world, and it is all because of rock stars like Kaelin."

Tyler McCarthy
Kaelin's music teacher

"Having been a teacher for the past 20 years, I can't begin to explain how rare it is to work with a student like Kaelin. Her smile lights up a room, and her dedication, persistence, and love of learning shines through in all that she does in the classroom. Kaelin is an avid reader and accomplished author. It is inspiring to see her novels come together at such a young age. She has completed nine novels to date! Kaelin writes because it's what she loves to do, and that is something we can all be inspired by: she fearlessly pursues what sets her soul on fire. She is living proof that anxiety goes out the window when we are doing what we love."

Rachele Tancredi
Kaelin's teacher

To Feel is to Love,
To Love is to Grow,
Expanding yourself out to others,
feel the ripple effect of your Energy.
The expansion of Self to others, deep connections.
Like the never ending flow of the river that meets the ocean thats depths are infinite.
To Feel is to truly Live,
Letting in the warmth to the deepest part of our existence.
That place that holds the spark of our Being.
Without Love, the spark will surely be extinguished.
Let others in to the place of vulnerability to stoke your flame.
In doing this, your heart and Love open to all others.
You feel the expansion and wonder of your true self bursting forth like the butterfly
from its cocoon.
The colours and vibrancy of your True Self is beyond all you can imagine,
You Are Love.

Zengirl

HELP YOUR HEROES

Want to help make the world a better place, but don't know how?
Help our Canadian heroes with some volunteer work or a small donation to their
organizations, or to charities they support!

HUNGER

Give a Free Lunch – Issabella, Mackenzie, Amelia, and Kaeden Patel
http://www.giveafreelunch.com

Maya Kooner supports the Riley Park Garden and the Mount Pleasant Neighbourhood
House (Vancouver, BC)

ANIMAL WELLNESS

Jade Peter supports the Humane Society, the Sandy Pines Wildlife Centre, and the
Napanee Community Kitten Rescue (Napanee, ON)

ENVIRONMENT

The Green Hope Foundation – Kehkashan Basu
http://greenhopefoundation.wixsite.com/greenhope

Save The Earth Man (S.T.E.M.) – Mushahid Khan

DISEASES AND DISABILITIES

Cuddles for Cancer – Faith Dickinson
http://cuddlesforcancer.ca

SK8 for ALS – Cole Hayward
@sk8forals2017
www.facebook.com/sk8forals

Happy Soul Project – Pip
https://www.shophappysoulproject.com

Gypsie – Meriel Reed

https://gypsiegirl13.wixsite.com/gypsie

Spectrum Acres – Jeron Van Dyk
https://www.facebook.com/spectrumacres/

ALS Canada, supported by Cole Hayward

Children's Wish Foundation, supported by Jax McMackin

The Therapeutic Clown Program, supported by Jax McMackin and Abby Springham

Easter Seals, supported by Harley Moon

The Sturge-Weber Foundation, supported by Harley Moon

Brantford Walk for a Cure, supported by Avery Plumb

The Abby Fund, supported by Meriel Reed

Toronto Sick Kids, supported by Abby Springham

Children's Hospital (London, ON), supported by Abby Springham

WELLNESS

Zach Makes Tracks – Zachary Hofer
https://zachmakestracks.ca

Go Girls, supported by Sarah Chisholm

Yellow Ribbon Campaign and Treats for Troops, supported by Faith Dickinson

Roots and Wings (Kingston, ON), supported by Abby Fitzpatrick

The Helping Us Understand Grief program in the Matthew's House Hospice (Tottenham, ON) and The Push for Change, supported by Michael Foster

The Child and Youth Mental Unit at the Royal Victoria Regional Health Centre (Barrie, ON), supported by Zachary Hofer

Peace Tree International, supported by Mushahid Khan

Kill it With Kindness (Toronto, ON), supported by Celia, Annie,
and Aryana Siriopoulos

Heads Together, supported by Kaelin Woods

Love Peace Harmony Foundation supported by Gus Dallal, Elijah and Nephtalie Neplaz

Look for products from our heroes that you can use in your home or in a classroom!

Doogoods by Teagan Adams
http://doogoods.com/

***The Art of Appreciation: How to Appreciate Everything You Have and Take Nothing for Granted* by Sanjana Ambegaonkar**
http://youngmindsbigimpact.com/

***The Tree of Hope* by Kehkashan Basu**
https://www.amazon.ca/Tree-Hope-Kehkashan-Basu/dp/0956995527

***Take the Lead: 7 Easy Ways to Unleash Your Inner Voice* by Aura Chapdelain**
Scheduled release: September 2018

***Nowhere to Call Home: Photographs & Stories of the Homeless* series by Leah Denbok**
ldenbokphotography.ca
https://www.instagram.com/humanizing_the_homeless/

***The Secret Portal* by Mckenna Lumley**
https://www.facebook.com/secretportal/

Caardia (music)
https://www.caardia.com

Don't forget that May is the awareness month for:

Lyme disease (Casey DeMerchant)
Brain tumours (McKenna Lumley)
Sturge-Weber Syndrome (Harley Moon)

Mark your calendar for Make a Difference Day!
Fourth Saturday in October (Faith Dickinson)

Meet the Hero Intelligence Team!

Tammy Vallieres (Co-founder of The Compassionate Crew and The Compass of Life Social and Emotional Wellness Program) has come to realize that her pain and struggle through the school system was all part of a master plan to become a change agent in education today. Her own awakening enabled her to create the Classroom Transformation Master Class, a style of teaching that fosters the social and emotional wellness of children so they can become the everyday heroes that the world desperately needs. At the end of it all, they listen to their innate wisdom and learn to trust themselves to make good decisions for their desired future. She trusts that one day classrooms around the world will fully embrace the beauty that diversity, abilities, and differences bring to expand our hearts.

Jen Fitzpatrick, aka Jenny Fitz (Founder of FEMM International, Owner of Serendipity Studios) has an innate ability to create connections around the world. She has been called the "conduit", and one of her favourite pastimes is networking so she can learn more about what others are doing both personally and professionally. Being co-founder of the Hero Intelligence Agency has allowed for the connections to broaden and for Jen to participate in the beautiful unfolding of stories of incredible youth heroes, their mentors, and advocates. Jen knows the importance of listening to our youth and providing them with a safe, non-judgmental platform where they can use their voices to instill confidence in others.

Susan Howson (Founder of Kids Coaching Connection and Manifest Your Magnificence) believes that everyone is born perfect, whole, complete, creative, resourceful, and knowing, with a dream to be manifest in the world. She has devoted her life to helping kids and youth flourish; to connect to their hearts in order to reach their true magnificence. Susan teaches how to transform the mindsets of children and youth to one of boundless creation, highest potential, and alignment with their true selves. Like the kids and youth in this book, Susan's dream is that everyone will feel motivated to move forward with eagerness and conviction to create a life - and a world - filled with love, peace and harmony.

JB Owen (Founder and CEO of Lotus Liners and the visionary behind Lotuste') is passionate about inspiring the new generation of women to find their voice and be themselves. JB and her family are avid volunteers and community champions, completing an 11-month tour of nine countries to share the message of JUST GIVE TODAY, a non-profit organization created by her children to teach others that we can all give hugs, smiles and joy. She is an innovator megapreneur, prolific speaker and philanthropist, whose unwavering dedication to female and environmental causes has led her to build businesses, design products and create brands that make a difference in the lives of many and around the world.

Anastasia Saluk became interested in writing when she was seven-years-old. Her teacher encouraged creative writing, and as her initial career choice of becoming a mermaid was proving to be an unfeasible option, she thought to become a writer instead. In addition to her role with Hero Intelligence Agency, Anastasia is an author, teacher, tutor, and an actress, student, and instructor in her hometown.

SUPPORTING IDEAS & ACTIVITIES

The following activities are intended to create dialogue and through the use of imagination, the possibilities are endless! We invite you to try these with your children, classroom, co-workers, friends and or family. Enjoy!

Use the following questions to fill in the boxes below:

1. What is the dream in your heart?
2. How can we work together to create change?
3. What does your community need?
4. How can each person do their part to help others?
5. What things are you doing right now that are positive and helping others?
6. What challenges do you face when trying to reach our goals?
7. What do you envision for the future?
8. Who can help us achieve your goals?
9. What advice would you give to other youth/adults?

I AM_____

MY DREAM:

MY SUPERPOWER:

MY VOICE MATTERS:

MY HEROES ARE:

MY ADVICE:

YOU ARE A SUPERHERO! DRAW YOUR OWN VERSION OF YOUR SUPER-HERO SELF:

Acknowledgements

We are forever grateful for the support and encouragement from everyone who contributed in bringing life to this project! We have put our hearts and souls into creating a platform for youth heroes to share their courageous stories, and we know that this book is the vehicle to creating a more positive, accepting and compassionate world. We would like to mention a few special people who have worked tirelessly over the last year to create a finished product that we are all extremely proud of. Most of all, we are proud of the youth heroes who all have a story to tell. The Hero in US sees the Hero in YOU! The incredible editor, Anastasia Saluk, who worked tirelessly to connect with our youth heroes and their families and supporters, as well as the influencers featured throughout the book.

Canadian Icons and Heroes including Severn Cullis-Suzuki for providing the foreword and Rick Hansen for providing an inspirational quote and book review.

The unwavering support we have received from our beloved family and friends.

JB Owen for the beautiful cover design, as well as typesetting and designing the interior.

Photographers, including (but not limited to) Nicholas Theodorou and Scott Cooper, as well as many others who have provided incredible images of our youth heroes and contributors.

Influencers, mentors, teachers, coaches, parents, advocates and youth supporters who have contributed to the book by way of sharing their stories, and or positive feedback.

Global organizations that support our vision, our youth heroes, and the platform we have created through the Hero Intelligence Agency.

You, the reader, whose life will be forever changed after you read the incredible journeys of each of these YOUth heroes.